Praise for *The Intimacy You Crave*

"This book will revolutionize y[   ]boost!"

    –Dr. Kevin Leman, author of *Sheet Music* and *Have a Happy Family by Friday*

"In a market that is filled with books that are sooo serious and formal, Lu sweeps in like that quirky, fun, irreverent big sister who can say anything and makes you blush. . .but who you might actually listen to. I think there will be women who read THIS type of book about sex who would never read the ones that are oh-so-serious."

    –Shaunti Feldhahn, social researcher and best-selling author of *For Women Only*

"I recently wrote a book called, *7 Ways to Be Her Hero: The One Your Wife Has Been Waiting For*. Everywhere I go, people will ask, 'What about a book for women on how to treat their husbands?' Well, it would have been wiser for me to write that one since women buy books on marriage, but I don't need to write it because Lucille Williams has done it. Every part I've read, I thought, 'Wow! That's good. That's bold. That's so darn helpful.' I'm excited to see this get published, I'm excited to promote it, and I'm excited for my wife to read it and share it with her friends. Many of the painful marriages that we're hearing about could be solved with Lucille's wisdom and challenges."

    –Doug Fields, author of 50+ books, including *7 Ways to Be Her Hero: The One Your Wife Has Been Waiting For, Getting Ready for Marriage*, and *The First Few Years of Marriage* (with Jim Burns). See more at dougfields.com

"Imagine having a conversation about sex over coffee with a wonderful mentor who is fun, funny, unashamedly Christian, and blunt! That's what you will experience with this book. As a man reading, *The Intimacy You Crave*, I smiled often and thought 'preach it sister' even more often. Lu Williams is an amazing woman who makes the subject of sex, which can seem awkward, incredibly delightful and God-honoring. I loved the book and am so thankful that Lu has a deep passion to safeguard marriages."

    –Jim Burns, PhD, President, HomeWord, author of *The Purity Code* and *Doing Life with Your Adult Children: Keep Your Mouth Shut and the Welcome Mat Out*

"Bold, loving, and humble are words that come to mind when I think of Lucille Williams. Her life is a testimony to Christ in how she has loved her family, pursued friendships, and invested herself in others' lives. If you want to deepen your understanding and commitment to your marriage, this book

...is a must-read! No matter how long you've been married, you'll be compelled to reexamine your marriage relationship and spice it up!"

—Caleb Kaltenbach, Founder of The Messy Grace Group
and author of *Messy Grace* and *God of Tomorrow*

"I so much appreciate Mike and Lucille Williams! They are both open, honest and real. In *The Intimacy You Crave*, Lucille brings that same authentic and transparent attitude to a topic that frankly scares people, and she does so in a relevant way. This book is a must-read for every married couple no matter what age. Through entertaining and humorous stories, Lucille breaks down the awkwardness that can loom while discussing the topic of sex. I highly recommend this book!"

—Craig Jutila, President Empowering Living Inc.,
author of *Faith and the Modern Family*

"I wish I had this book in the early years of my marriage as I struggled to deprogram my mind from what the world says sex is and reprogram it according to the Word of God. Every wife and engaged woman needs this book in her library. Shackles will fall off as wives turn each page. This book is a breath of fresh air. It's liberating, empowering, and funny! Thank you, Lu, for your boldness and for this anointed work."

—Monique Robinson, Ordained Minister, author of *Longing for Daddy*

"Lu writes with wisdom and passion as she offers women no excuses to shrink away or disregard the sexual relationship with their spouse. She instead encourages and writes about both the mental and physical components of sex and offers biblical counsel in a real, humorous, and no-nonsense approach that will keep you laughing and engaged the whole way through."

—Cindy Marston, Director of Women's Encounters, Shepherd Church

"I have been privileged to witness [Lucille's] relationship with her husband and have seen their healthy, fun, respectful marriage. Her lighthearted approach makes you feel like you're at a local coffee shop, while the content leaves you as though you just went through years of counseling. She is honest, she is relatable, she is real."

—Amanda Boddeker, Admissions Counselor at Dallas Theological Seminary

"The topic of sex within marriage carries with it such secrecy and a hush-hush attitude within much of the church, even today. And yet, it's so widely exploited in media and so important in relationships. Lucille tackles this topic in true 'Lucille-style.' She's open, honest, transparent, and definitely does not beat around the bush. Wives will benefit from this life applicable book."

—Kathie Pisano, Pastor's Wife, Real Life Church

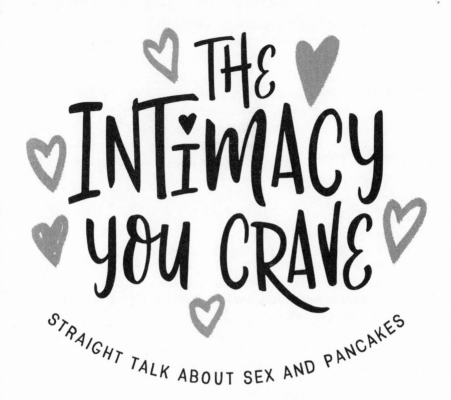

THE INTIMACY YOU CRAVE

STRAIGHT TALK ABOUT SEX AND PANCAKES

LUCILLE WILLIAMS

SHILOH RUN PRESS
An Imprint of Barbour Publishing, Inc.

Published in association with the literary agency of Credo Communications, LLC, Grand Rapids, Michigan, www.credocommunications.net.

Scripture taken from the New American Standard Bible, © 1960, 1962, 1963, 1968, 1971, 1972, 1973, 1975, 1977, 1995 by The Lockman Foundation. Used by permission.

Cover design: Greg Jackson, Thinkpen Design; thinkpendesign.com

Published by Shiloh Run Press, an imprint of Barbour Publishing, Inc., 1810 Barbour Drive, Uhrichsville, Ohio 44683, www.shilohrunpress.com

Our mission is to inspire the world with the life-changing message of the Bible.

Member of the
Evangelical Christian
Publishers Association

Printed in the United States of America.

CONTENTS

SISTER, YOU'VE COME TO THE RIGHT PLACE!

I am so happy you picked up this book! This is the part where I convince you not to put it down but to read it. That decision, my new friend, is entirely up to you, but I sincerely want you to stay because we have an adventure to take. A sex adventure. Did I say that out loud? Ha! No, I just wrote it, but I said it out loud in my head. Does that count?

Sex is fun! So a book about sex should be fun too. That's why I'll frequently use fun phrases for sex throughout the pages that follow. I want you to know what they are ahead of time so that we're singing from the same love-song sheet. Cue "Endless Love."

Fun Expressions Referring to Sex
- Makin' bacon
- Basket making
- Baking the potato
- Sexy time
- Bedroom rodeo
- Play zone
- Fun time
- Washing clothes
- Sweaty yoga
- Hot date
- Jousting
- Taking the magic bus to Manchester
- Taking Grandma to Applebee's
- Buying Frisbees

- Buttering the biscuit
- Shrimpin' the barbie
- Banana-in-the-fruit-salad
- Playing poker
- Shampooing the wookie
- Bam-bam in the ham
- Bow-chick-a-wow-wow
- Hot pudding for supper
- Joint session of Congress
- Adult nap time
- Churning butter
- Moving furniture
- Horizontal tango
- Marital congress
- Horizontal refreshments
- Mattress dancing
- Matrimonial polka
- Opening the gates of Mordor
- Dancing in the sheets
- Gettin' jiggy with it
- Hanky-panky
- Boom-boom
- Rockin' and rollin'
- Jiving
- Taking a roll
- Bouncy-bouncy
- Playtime
- Driving Miss Daisy
- Waka-waka
- Monster mash
- Horizontal hokeypokey
- Diddle-diddle

- Interior decorating
- Sexual congress
- Jingle-jangle time
- Getting busy
- Slippin' and slidin'
- Baking lasagna
- Parallel parking
- Amorous congress
- Monkey business
- Tumbling

If the Title Sparks Uneasiness

I don't know about you, but anytime I read books about sex, I'm a bit uncomfortable about others seeing what I'm reading. *Don't look at what I'm reading—it's none of your beeswax.* So if you're anything like me, I'd like to give you permission to add a false cover to this book or at least put a sticker over the word *sex.* I understand. You have my blessing. Now you're free to roam around without feeling self-conscious.

On the other hand, if you're one of those women who totally rolls with it when your kid is throwing a fit in the grocery store or speaks up when someone cuts in line, display this book on your coffee table, carry it to the gym, take it to church, and read it in line at your local coffeehouse.

And please, if *The Intimacy You Crave* helps you, tell your friends—tell everyone! I want this book to help as many marriages as possible.

Why I Have Written This Book and Why It Will Help You

I have a passion to safeguard marriages. Being married to a children's pastor, I've witnessed countless hurting children affected by divorce. I've seen firsthand the pain not only in the eyes of the children but also in their parents. A family torn apart is devastation beyond words.

The sexual relationship between husband and wife is the beating heart of marriage. Sexual intimacy bonds this God-ordained union and sets it apart from every other earthly relationship. A healthy, happy sex life and marital bond secures a family. If this book can put even a tiny dent in the divorce rate, helping even just one couple, it can affect an entire tribe. One family can change future generations for eternity. I pray that family is yours.

Please Understand

There are exceptions to everyone and everything. Please keep this truth in mind as you read. There's no 100 percent, all the time, except when it comes to God.

Anonymous Husbands

Throughout these pages, you will find real quotes from real men, though names have been changed to protect the innocent. Each quote begins with "What he wants you to know," because it's stuff husbands would like their wives to know.

Secret Sex Missions

At the close of each chapter is a Secret Sex Mission challenge. Complete the twelve challenges and help safeguard your marriage and begin the road to a happier and healthier you, marriage, and sex life.

Ask Him

Also at the close of each chapter is a question or two to help open dialogue between you and your husband. Please take advantage of these suggestions and get all you can from *The Intimacy You Crave*.

A Little Confession

Before we continue, I want to make a little confession of sorts. I was talking with my husband at a coffeehouse and asked, "Can you believe I've written a book about sex?"

To which he replied, "I *know*! And you're such a prude."

Truth be told, I really am a bit of a prude. I get embarrassed every time someone talks about sex. I'd really rather let people think I was celibate than in a thriving sexual relationship. Each time I was pregnant, I felt like people were looking at me and thinking, *I know what you did.* When my kids got wind that "something was going on with Mom and Dad" and my daughter gave me that teasing look of "I know what you were doing," I felt embarrassed and wanted to lie about it. When my husband says, "Thanks for the great time," I blush. Every. Time. When we are in a public place and he looks at me intently and says, "You're hot," I reply with, "Shhhhhh." So if anything in these pages causes you to blush—girlfriend, I'm blushing with you.

Now, shall we get moving?

PART 1

STRAIGHT TALK

CHAPTER 1

LET'S TALK ABOUT SEX

> NOT TONIGHT, HONEY—
> I HAVE A HEADACHE.

There was no possibility of escaping the awkwardness. It was one of those times when you wish you could have a do-over, but you've dug yourself a hole and your only choice is to sit in it while spectators watch your little circus act.

Yeah, one of *those* moments.

I was a highly enthusiastic, brand-spanking-new Christian, and my husband was shiny new as well. And what do you do when you've just become a Christian? Well, you join a Bible study, of course. We were in our early twenties, BK (before kids), zealous rookie followers of Jesus, and the home Bible study we joined was led by an elder in our new church. We were right out of the gate big-time!

We loved attending each week and loved the warm, welcoming, and sincere group of people. There were newly married couples all the way on up to grandmas and grandpas. They all seemed to have a handle on how to live a Christian life, and we so wanted to emulate these seasoned, God-loving believers.

Oh, and one last important detail: this was an extremely conservative group. Think of the most conservative Christians you've ever met and double it. Okay, now we're on the same page.

Yes, we truly enjoyed going. Until one night. . .

After the Bible lesson, the elder who was leading our study opened the floor—actually, it was a big circle—for comments and application. My hand shot up. I had been reading a book and wanted to share a story about a fighter pilot. I was nervous but really wanted to be embraced by the group. After being given permission to speak, I hesitantly proceeded with my story.

The more I spoke, the more I got into my groove, dramatically increasing my enthusiasm. When I got to the part in the story where the fighter pilot ejected out of his plane, that's when things took a turn for the worst.

"He ejaculated out of the plane!" I exclaimed. *Ejaculated?* Something didn't sound right.

"Ejaculated?" I repeated it several times: "Ejaculated. Ejaculated? He ejaculated out of the plane?" And if that wasn't bad enough, I had hand motions to go with my story. (Come on, who talks without their hands?) So, as I said "ejaculated," my hands were sweeping around the room in increasingly embarrassing ways.

The room was dead silent.

My husband buried his head in his hands, obviously wishing he were Houdini and could somehow escape.

Prolonging my circus act. . .

The leader of the study simply stated, "Eject."

Having finally been given the right word, I continued, "Yeah, eject. The pilot ejected out of the plane." Awkwardly, I proceeded to finish my story with all the finesse I could muster, but it was too late; finesse died at "ejaculation."

Not one person laughed or even let out a chuckle. No one said a word. Not then, or ever.

As we were leaving the study, my husband muttered to me under his breath, "We are never coming back." And we never did.

Shhhh! Don't Talk about It

Don't talk about such things! was the message we took away from that Bible study episode. C'mon, people. Laugh! That's funny! So today—and throughout this book—we *are* going to talk about such things. Are you ready to talk about sex? And maybe laugh a little too, or laugh a lot? You've read this far; decide right now that you are going to read all the way through. I don't know your reasons for picking up this book. Maybe you have a great sex life and want to improve it. Fantastic! Maybe your sex life is less than you'd like it to be or perhaps even so terrible you don't even want to think about it. In any case, this book is for you. Perhaps your relationship could use more passion, more sizzle, more spice. If so, you've come to the right place.

Do you want to have a great sex life with your husband? I adamantly believe great sex makes life great. I know it makes *my* life great. When things are right in the bedroom, life is better—feelings of love, security, and contentment infuse me. I feel like I'm walking around with a little smile on my face all the time.

You may be thinking, *Come on! Can fireworks and excitement in the bedroom really be sustained over many years with kids and work and all of life's problems?* All I know is that as I write this, I have been continually distracted by texts coming in from my husband that. . .well. . .let's just say I'm not at liberty to share. Are we newlyweds? Nope. As I write this, we've been married for more than thirty-six years, and our marriage just keeps getting better and better—in every way.

Was my marriage always this way? No, it wasn't. In fact, there was a time many years ago when I would have described my marriage as downright rotten. Really rotten! Frankly, there were days when I would ask myself, "What did I do?" and "How much longer can I go on like this?"

As many women do who are in struggling marriages, I thought the majority of our problems were mostly because of *him*. Over and over in my head, I would replay the "wrongs" I had "suffered" from my husband.

When I decided I was going to change things, I got real honest with God. And then I got real honest with myself. Honesty hurts sometimes, but God showed that it was *me* who had the majority of changing to do. I decided then and there that I can't change my husband, but I *can* change me. God showed me that I had to pull up my sleeves—and a few other things—and get serious about being the best wife I could be. Especially the best wife I could be in the bedroom.

In the end, do you know who got to benefit from that paradigm shift? Me! God's ways are always better than our ways. Infinitely better. And this goes for the bedroom too.

Today I can honestly and wholeheartedly say that I am contentedly and blissfully married. That may sound sappy, but it's true. I can only attribute this transformation to God, who brought it about as I gave up my selfish ways in exchange for His more perfect ways. As a result, I am in a happy, thriving, and passionate marriage. Like any other couple, we have had and continue to have struggles, but we use them to make us stronger. We fight—fiercely—to keep our marriage all that God crafted it to be, though we have plenty of normal conflicts too.

Tackling conflict and struggle together strengthens and unifies us, building trust and commitment. We have learned to put the other first: "Through the grace given to me I say to everyone among you not to think more highly of himself than he ought to think; but to think so as to have sound judgment, as God has allotted to each a measure of faith" (Romans 12:3). Giving up self through trust enhances our physical relationship. It keeps the passion alive.

That, my friend, is God's plan. It is God's plan that you keep your marriage strong—in every way. God will use your marriage to honor Him: "Be devoted to one another in brotherly love;

give preference to one another in honor; not lagging behind in diligence, fervent in spirit, serving the Lord" (Romans 12:10-11). Who is your closest "brother"? Your husband, of course! When we honor and serve our husbands, we are serving the Lord. Have you ever thought of it like that? As we do the work that a happy, thriving, and steamy marriage requires, God will chisel away at us and shape us into the best version of ourselves.

Marriage is a chisel God uses to create a masterpiece.

Moreover, keeping the marriage bed sacred and flourishing is a part of God's plan—and worth fighting for. Amen?

God designed sex, and it truly is a mystery—two becoming one. It is the lifeblood of the family. Sex bonds husband and wife and creates offspring. How God creates children from the union of husband and wife is simply a miracle. And above all else, God created sex for our pleasure. "The man and his wife were both naked and were not ashamed" (Genesis 2:25). They were naked and unashamed—unashamed of the pleasure they felt in being *together*. All God's design.

Except. . .Women Really Do Want to Talk about It

"Lu, can I talk with you?"

"Absolutely!" My friend and ministry teammate, Camille (not her real name—most names have been changed), served the Lord faithfully and had an exemplary marriage. I was more than happy to sit down with her.

"Lu, I'm a virgin." *What?* I thought to myself. *She and her husband have two beautiful little girls. She's messing with me.*

"Um, Camille, what are you talking about?"

"My husband and I haven't had sex in over eight years."

I began to laugh. *She really got me this time. I know her husband, and he's a wonderful man. They have a great marriage. Wait, she's not laughing with me. Oh no, she's serious! Oh no, oh no, oh no! I just laughed at her. I'm a terrible pastor's wife.* (Oh yeah, did I mention that God turned my wannabe-escape-artist-husband into a pastor? God really does work in ways we don't understand.)

"Camille, are you serious?"

"Yes."

"I am so sorry. Please forgive me." My jaw was dropping in my mind.

Camille gracefully said, "It's okay." Luckily for me, she is not one to be easily offended.

I was astonished. Shocked. Taken aback. *This just can't be true; it just can't be! Yikes, so what she means is that she feels like a virgin all over again. I think that may be even worse. Take a big breath. Quick prayer: Lord God, please give me wisdom.*

"I thought you were joking. You both seem to have a great marriage."

"No, it stinks. Lu, I'm at the end of my rope. If this doesn't change, I want to leave him."

So much for how things look.

"Whoa. Wow. Whoa. Hold on there. You can fix this. I will help you." From that day forward, Camille and her husband embarked on a mission to repair their marriage—*in every way.* Today they continue to work on their marriage, but both Camille and her husband are glad she decided to stick it out, and I'm sure their two girls would say it has been worth it. Despite all they've been through, Camille once again sees her husband for the good man he is—a man who loves God and loves his family—and she is proud to be married to him.

Why do I share Camille's story here? Since I started this project and have shared it with multiple women, the response has been overwhelming. When they hear what I'm writing about, they jump at the opportunity to talk. *About sex.* "Make sure you talk about this. . . . And don't forget about such and such. . . .

And you know many couples have trouble with. . ." Occasionally I've heard things that have really surprised me, but more than anything, listening to these women and their stories has inspired me to continue. I really thought that the majority of people who were married had a decent sex life, or at least a somewhat adequate sex life, and that those who got divorced were the ones who had trouble. Boy, was I wrong! Many couples are really struggling, and many are in sexless marriages. How very sad.

But what is even sadder is that they so often keep it to themselves, too embarrassed to tell anyone. I've found this to be the case as I have counseled many different women over the years. When I started this project and women heard about my writing venture, their stories came flooding in—some happy but, unfortunately, many unhappy. My prayer is that the subject of sex would become more acceptable to discuss in the church, and more specifically, that younger women would feel comfortable going to older women: "Older women likewise are to be reverent in their behavior, not malicious gossips nor enslaved to much wine, teaching what is good, so that they may encourage the young women to love their husbands, to love their children, to be sensible, pure, workers at home, kind, being subject to their own husbands, so that the word of God will not be dishonored" (Titus 2:3–5).

The Church Needs to Start Talking

One newly married pastor's wife told me their wedding night was far from what they had hoped it would be. She and her husband had waited until marriage, and they had garrisoned their expectations with premarital counseling as well. Nonetheless, the night they had been waiting for with high anticipation turned out to be a disaster. "I wish our premarital counseling had prepared us better," she told me with a pained look. "It was awful." And if that wasn't enough, her husband felt terrible about the whole experience, feeling like he failed her. Not exactly the best way to start off your marriage.

During courtship is when couples seem the most open to premarital guidance and counsel, which is why my premarital book, *From Me to We*, covers eighty-eight discussion questions every couple needs to tackle preferably before they say, "I do."

Bob Berkowitz, PhD, and Susan Yager-Berkowitz, in their book *He's Just Not Up for It Anymore*, discuss how young girls learn about romance at an early age. Many young women carry into marriage an unrealistic idea about the magical and romantic adventure their honeymoon and first night together will be. Unfortunately, the reality is that some don't even consummate their marriage. After such high expectations, the disappointment can be traumatic, leaving the new bride with feelings of deep dissatisfaction. She thinks her situation is unique and therefore doesn't talk to anyone to avoid further embarrassment.[1]

We need to equip our newly married couples—and old married couples—with the best tools possible, giving them the best shot at marital paradise. Unfortunately, few get good hot and spicy sex advice before they take the walk down the aisle. (Chapter 2 will cover this subject more fully.)

But we in the church have the secret ingredient for great sex. We have the owner's manual! Our secret ingredient: God. The owner's manual: the Bible. *Sex was God's idea.* Look in your Bible; God talks about sex. A lot, actually. If God talks about sex, we can talk about sex too. Get out your Bible and read the Song of Solomon with a friend. You'll both be blushing in minutes! The reason I am talking so much about God in this first chapter is because many think God is anti-sex. He is not.

Here's the simple equation: sex is in the Bible; hence, we talk about it. If anyone should be having great sex, it's those of us who know God personally. Please understand me here: I'm not saying you should share intimate details about your sex life with random strangers. Uh, no! But help a sister out if she could use some advice on keeping romance alive in her marriage. Maybe that sister is you.

So why don't we in the church talk about sex more? How refreshing would it be to see the word *sex* in the church bulletin? Let's Talk about Sex Group, Wednesdays at 8:00 p.m. Hold the applause—I'm joking—but it is time the church talked about sex a bit more. After all, the church should be the one place that couples—*married* couples—go to get the best sex advice around.

Regrettably, many times the first sexual encounter young women hear about is the "mess-up" one or more of their friends had. A Christian friend goes outside of God's design and has sex before marriage, and then she shares that disappointing experience with her trusted friend. Or even worse, they hear about the many sexual escapades their non-Christian friends are having. Then when they have questions, they go to their "experienced" friends for advice. This gives them a contaminated view of the wonderful gift of sex. Sadly, too many of us start our sex lives this way: with stories from our friends that are tarnished and not the story God has for us.

I know this was my daughter's experience, except that she fortunately came to me with her questions. "Mom, does it hurt? Monique said it hurt—a lot. And Angela said it's hot, sweaty, and really short." (Doesn't that make you want to hop in the sack? Sheesh.) I was able to explain to her that anytime we go outside of God's design, especially with regard to our sexual purity, it is not going to be the special gift God intended it to be.

If this is you, don't despair. God can and will restore you.

"Wash me, and I shall be whiter than snow," we read in Psalm 51:7. Understand that sexuality is something God created, and the human sex drive is extremely strong—more for some than for others. Many would go without food, sleep, and basic necessities in exchange for a romp in the play zone. My point being, if this is an area where you have taken a mistake from your past and carried it into your present, let it go. You are not defined by a mistake in your past, and if you've given it to God, He does not hold it against you. You are free to fully embrace and enjoy your husband physically. (We'll talk more about this throughout these pages.)

Woefully, the message young people receive in the church is also "Don't talk about sex." We tell them, "Don't, don't, don't," "It's wrong," "God says no," "Wait until marriage," "Keep your pants zipped." These messages are laced with good intentions, but ultimately many of them do far more harm than good.

At our church, our middle school and high school ministries do an excellent job of teaching and explaining to kids what God says about sex before marriage and the dangers it presents outside of marriage. But what about *after* they're married? Where's the message saying, "Go! Go all out! Knock your socks off!" Maybe we need to add a new element to the wedding ceremony where the preacher says something like, "By the power vested in me by the almighty God, I want you both to go back to the room you will share tonight and enjoy each other with reckless abandon. This is a direct order from God. And don't ever stop until Jesus comes back."

All right, maybe the preacher wouldn't say all that. But someone needs to tell them! Don't you think so? Did anyone ever say that to you? During church announcements—in between the baptism class and home group sign-ups—let's add, "For all you married folks out there, go home and 'appreciate' your spouse with some 'fun.' And for all you married ladies who came to church alone today, go home and love on your man. Tell him, 'I don't know what it is about church, but it gets my engine running!' We'll save a seat for him next week." Where's that message? If we could get that message out, our churches would be overflowing with happy men and women, and happy, *steamy* marriages.

Now that we've landed on *steamy*, let's talk about making *your* marriage steamy and electric, shall we? You may not agree with all that I express, and you may even be offended at times. That is not my objective. More than anything, I want you to know my goal in writing is to enhance your marriage. A great sex life is a critical part of a great marriage—a marriage reflecting the goodness of God in which you and your husband give yourselves to each other in body, mind, and soul.

I am so excited about the journey we're about to embark on together. Will you join me? Do you want to give your marriage a boost? Do you want to enhance your sex life? Are you ready to do more basket making? (If that didn't make sense, please go back and check out the "Read This First" section.) Join me! Read to the end of this book, and let's do this—we're just getting started.

SECRET SEX MISSION #1

This is your mission if you wish to accept it: Get honest with yourself and God. Take some time to think about your marriage and ask yourself what areas need changing. Is your intimate time together all you wish it were? Spend some time in prayer asking God to show you where you can use improvement in this area. Completing this first mission will set you up for success.

ASK HIM

How did you and your husband each learn about sex? What messages—expressed and implied—about sexuality did you receive from your parents and your childhood church? How have these messages shaped your view of sex in marriage today?

CHAPTER 2

YOU'RE ABOUT TO BE MARRIED, SO LET'S TALK TURKEY ABOUT ORGASMS

> NOT TONIGHT, HONEY— WE'RE NOT MARRIED YET.

My friend Carol asked me to lunch, and we chose one of my favorite restaurants. A quiet and quaint mom-and-pop with fantastic food. Once inside I noticed a gentleman at one of the four tables in the dining area working diligently on his laptop. And no matter how diligent and focused he was, I'm sure he paused when *we* entered the restaurant. "I'm going to talk about orgasms," Carol blurted out, "and I don't care if this guy hears about my orgasms—I'm going to talk about it anyway." *Wait. What? You don't care. But maybe I care?*

As we sat down, she continued, "I never had an orgasm before I was married." *Alrighty, friends, this roller coaster has left the station, and I think I'm on it, embarrassed or not. Don't look toward the guy; eye contact would make this even more awkward.* I tried to pretend he wasn't there and paid attention to her words, which were going to get even more interesting—and even more awkward. If that was even possible! Carol continued, "Then, *after* I was married, I *still* didn't have an orgasm. We would have sex, but it still didn't happen." *Gulp. Oh boy. I hope this guy's so into his work that he's not listening. Don't look, don't look.* She continued, "I felt very dissatisfied and unhappy with my sex life. Then Glen taught me how to touch myself while we were together, and it finally happened. So that's what I would do." *Is the story over? Can we move on now? Breathe.*

Carol kept going: "This is something that needs to be talked about. Most women don't have an orgasm during intercourse, and they may think there's something wrong with them. I know I didn't know if it was normal or not. I even told this story at my women's Bible study, and many women could relate." *Now that's a Bible study I want to join. Sounds like a vibrant group.* Back to Carol: "After I talked about it, many other women said they'd had the same experience, and they were happy to hear what I had to say. It made them feel not only normal, but not alone, and understood. It's lonely when your sex life isn't all you had hoped it would be. Someone needs to talk about this. You need to talk about this." *I think the ride stopped. Can we talk about anything other than orgasms? I think the waitstaff, the restaurant owner, and this poor guy trying to work might be relieved this conversation is over.*

"So," Carol said after a pause, "how's Mike doing?" *Whew! Did that guy leave? [Quick peek.] Nope, still there.*

After the initial shock and awe wore off, I thought about it and decided that, yes, this does need to be talked about because a healthy, happy sex life is important, and God cares about it too. He cares about you, and He cares about your marriage *and* your sex life.

During a meeting my husband and I had with a prominent family pastor of a large church, this pastor talked about a class he conducted for premarital couples. At the close of the class, he ended his prayer with, "And Lord, give these couples great sex." Loud gasps came from several women in the room. My best guess is they hadn't heard that before. How could a pastor say such a thing? Because this pastor knows that God cares about your sex life, and God wants it to be all He created it to be. And it needs to be beyond amazing, just like the Creator intended.

If for some reason, and this will not *necessarily* be the case, you have intimacy problems right out of the gate, don't let them continue. Take action and do something about them. And for those of you who have been married for many years and think there's no hope, allow me to encourage you. You *can* turn things around; all it takes is some effort, patience, and knowledge. Don't be discouraged.

Please hear this again, and allow it to sink in: God wants you to be happy in your marriage, and especially in your sex life. Hebrews 13:4 instructs us, "Marriage is to be held in honor among all, and the marriage bed is to be undefiled; for fornicators and adulterers God will judge." The Greek word for "undefiled" is *amiantos*, as in unsoiled or pure. Just google "What does God say about sex?" and numerous verses will pop up. God talks about sex from Genesis to Revelation; He created the marriage union and wants us to be well equipped—and even to be experts. Experts. How many experts do I have out there? Can I get an "Amen"? What makes one an expert? If you've done something for one thousand hours. . . Never mind. Let's move on.

Where can young women go for straight talk about what to expect on their wedding night? While this book is for all women, I am dedicating *this* chapter to every woman soon to be married and to those who wish to be married in the future.

If you are already married, read on. If nothing else, perhaps I can take you back to your first-time experience with your husband. You may have a few laughs or, even better, get a jolt of sexual energy you can use on your husband later. This chapter is a bit of a detour reminiscing back to the beginning of your marriage. For you seasoned veterans, come with me back to a time when your ideas about sex and marriage were idealistic and fresh, a time when life was new and exciting. You were about to venture into the unknown world of married people, and everything was exhilarating.

Let's talk turkey about sex and "that special night."

My first tip on this topic is to read this whole book. If you have thumbed through the pages and landed on this chapter because you are getting married, great, but don't just read this chapter. The rest of the book will be just as important for you. There's no way I can cover it all in just one chapter. And please don't stop there: I invite you to pick up a copy of my book *From Me to We*, which covers more on this subject as well as many other valuable treasures for your life as husband and wife. And each chapter includes critical discussion questions you can tackle as a couple.

For now, let's get back to sex, orgasms, and that first night. There are a slew of complications that could turn what should be a hallelujah party into a half-baked chicken. Endometriosis, fibroid tumors, cysts, vaginismus (vaginal muscle spasms), and allergic reaction to contraception (such as condoms) are just a few ways your body could mess with you and mess up your fun. I don't want this chapter to be about what could go wrong, and I definitely don't want to scare you; I merely want you to be informed. Don't create drama or trauma where there most likely won't be any. And if, a big *IF* here, you have pain during intercourse—I've heard of couples not consummating their marriage due to painful intercourse; it's rare but it happens—and this pain prevents you from enjoying "traditional sex," it's time to get creative. Everyone can still reach the *boom!*—intercourse is not the only way. There are many ways to get there, so don't let painful intercourse stop your fun.

Nonetheless, if you find yourself needing help, get it. The medical field has advanced tremendously and continues to do so—vaginal dilators are even available now. Get the help you need for success.

You must get that chicken back in the oven.

Sometimes the answer to painful intercourse is a lubricant. You can get some just about anywhere. Getting married? Be prepared. Make this purchase. If you think you'll have sex, well, let's see. . .two, three, four times in your first week, have some lubricant with you. Actually, no, if you plan on having sex even just *one* time, have some. Make sure it's tucked in with your toothbrush. If you have a choice between a toothbrush and some lube, take the lube.

The Big Night

We get married and we expect the wedding night to be better than our favorite chick flick, romance novel, and summer night daydreams all rolled into one. You may have a vision of him carrying you over the threshold while kissing you with an unyielding thirst. The passion is so intense that you barely make it to the bed, and by the time you do, most of your clothes are already off. The electricity builds, and you are ready for him with an eagerness that surpasses all feelings you have ever experienced. The night is filled with apex after apex and for hours your life is a magical world of unending bliss.

Girl! We need to pause your sexy-time playlist and talk probabilities. I do applaud your zeal, however; keep playin' that playlist.

Please understand, most women have high expectations for their wedding night, which is totally normal and reasonable. Recognize that there are expectations, and then there is reality. Your reality will be unique to you and your husband. Every person is an individual, and your physical relationship with your husband will be uniquely yours as a couple. It will be built and shaped as you nurture this part of your adventure together. All yours. Special. Gold. Top. Best. Constructed specifically by you and your Mr. McDreamy. Never stop building your distinctive love tower, making it everything you wish. As with all parts of your marriage, this too will take time and effort. Hopefully the most enjoyable time and effort.

It all begins with a certain mind-set.

Let's Back It Up for a Bit

Why are you getting married? You love him, you say. Does he love you? Does he make you feel like a princess? Does he go out of his way for you? Does he spend long hours talking with you? Does he make you happy? Is he there when you need a shoulder to cry on? Are you two peas in a pod, tackling life together? Is it you and him against the world? Well, let me ask you another question: Who wouldn't love someone with all of those qualities? He sounds wonderful. He sounds charming. He sounds like your prince.

But let's get real, Cinderella.

Marriage is messy. People are messy and broken and flawed, and marriage will be the same way. There will be days when you feel as though you're the only one giving in your relationship, and you'll feel given out. (All you grammar experts out there, yes, I know *given* is not in the dictionary, but *given out* describes this feeling to a tee.) Given out. Those in successful marriages know that when you feel given out, this is exactly when the magic can happen in your relationship, if you can be the Energizer bunny and keep giving.

Marriage is about serving another.

Likewise, our sexual relationships are about giving. Giving unconditionally. Stop for a second. Marinate in this. Giving. Unconditionally. There will be times when the last thing you'll want to do is "be close." And yet you've pledged your life to another. As with the other parts of your marriage—in a thriving relationship—your sex life will be about serving the other. It's when we serve another that we feel the most fulfilled.

Does this mean you have to forfeit orgasms? No. No way! This means you work together for Team *Bang*—ecstasy for both players. Because his greatest pleasure will be to bring you pleasure. Most men—pretty much all—want to please their wives in all areas. And especially in the love boat. Don't believe me? Just ask him.

The truth is that for most women, orgasms take work. Some very fortunate few need no extra effort in this area. But for most, it's something you and your husband will need to discover, work at, and refine *together*. Many times you can be perfectly satisfied without reaching a climax, other times not so much. Learn how to navigate either scenario as a team. With him it's almost always a guarantee.

The female anatomy is designed in a somewhat fickle way. God planted a pleasure button within the female anatomy—it's called the clitoris. Find this pleasure button. Find it together. God put this button there. Why? To create pleasure for you. And for him.

Play God's exquisite creation. Think about a professional violinist. In the hands of the right musician, the violin creates beautiful music. There are different ways to play the violin in order to hit the right notes. Rhythmic strokes—slow, fast, soft, strong, gentle pulses, rapid reiteration—all create a lovely vibrato. The violinist commonly uses a bow but also plucks the strings with his fingers and strikes the strings with the wooden side of the bow. The musician had to learn to play the violin. Your Mr. Mc-Dreamy becomes your violin player. There are many ways to hit the right notes. Explore those ways together as he becomes a proficient violin player with a vibrant vibrato. Every professional has to practice.

Practice. Practice. Practice.

Remember, there are many ways to reach the goal. Carol and Glen found a way that worked for them. Every musician plays differently, but know that every song will be so worth it. Not to mention, playing—and practicing—is fun.

You'll want him to keep making music—trust me on this—so consistently express your delight and appreciation of him no matter what happens.

In the meantime, here's a verse to ponder: "Awake, O north wind, and come, wind of the south; make my garden breathe out fragrance, let its spices be wafted abroad. May my beloved come into his garden and eat its choice fruits!" (Song of Solomon 4:16).

Afterward, always shout, "*Olé!*" Nah, I'm just kidding. Afterward, always go to the bathroom. You wouldn't want to get an infection. And take note: the vagina is self-lubricating, self-cleaning (this is why you need to urinate), and slow to warm up. If you do want to shout anything, make it, "Bravo!" Or your form of "bravo." He'll appreciate the praise. Encore, encore.

The next thing I want to tell you is to relax. I could just leave it at that and tell you to relax, or I could illustrate it for you. With a story. Hold on not too tight, breathe in, breathe out, count to twenty, and come with me to euphoria land. The sometimes self-forbidden world of the indulger.

Living in Euphoria Land

Laura woke and immediately chanted, "Thank You, God, for another day!" Laura was especially thankful for *this* day, having anticipated its arrival for weeks. She was going to be doing one of her favorite carefully planned activities, one she looked forward to even in between dates.

Springing out of bed with an inhale of the morning air cascading through her bedroom window, she felt God's extra-big smile gazing upon her, along with the sun's glow radiating through the rooftop. (Yes, I'm aware the sun doesn't radiate through a roof. Maybe her home has a sunroof? Yeah, let's say there's a sunroof—just go with me on this.) Stepping into the shower, as the pulsing water engulfed her body, she found herself daydreaming about the day ahead and almost forgot to rinse the conditioner out of her long brown hair.

In the car she had to stop herself from racing to her destination. Arriving at her scheduled time, she set about the first order of business: disrobing, neatly folding her clothes, and slipping into her luxurious, plush, oh-so-familiar Luxor robe. Cozy. Soft. Her body relaxed. She let out a sigh of excited expectancy and relief.

Dropping into a comfy chair, she put her feet up and relaxed even more. Waiting. Slow inhale. Big, anticipatory exhale. As she exhaled, her body released the leftover tension and stress hiding in her muscles. She was glad she remembered to bring a book by one of her favorite authors. Time to read seemed to elude her more each day. Waiting actually felt pleasurable. She flipped open her book. And waited. Not with a sense of urgency, but with a warm calm.

The gentle sound of her name jolted Laura from the pages.

She was on her feet. Walking to another room, she felt a peaceful eagerness. The scent of lavender permeated the air. The darkness felt serene. With ready enthusiasm, she slipped off her robe and lay down. She felt warm, snug, at ease. This was going to be the best hour of her day, without a doubt, and she was going to savor each moment and every single sensation. She hadn't felt this much passion in months.

The awaited first stroke grazed her shoulder. With every touch her body steeped in tranquil pleasure. Paying attention to each detail, she felt every caress take her to deeper and deeper levels of gratification. She entered a world without distraction or strife, only a harmonious calm. Oh, how she loved this world of utter enjoyment. She didn't want it to end. She soaked in every sensation, wanting to stay there as long as she could, basking in the delight of touch.

Returning to her second shower of the day, Laura reflected on her rendezvous. This shower felt completely different from her morning shower. This shower poured warmth and joy and the delight of indulgence around her.

Pampered. Precious. Maybe a little spoiled.

After carefully placing her clothes back on her refreshed body, she headed out. She walked taller, more confidently, feeling unruffled, undeterred.

"How was everything?" The girl at the counter was as cheerful as always. "Will it be cash or card today?"

The question jarred her from her refreshed and recharged state. "Card. And yes, it was wonderful."

"Next time you might like to try our hot stones. It's one of our most requested services. Would you like to schedule your next massage?"

Massage.

I love getting massages. Don't you? When I pamper myself in this way, I pay attention to every detail and fully indulge. You get where I'm going with this, right? What if it wasn't a massage? What if it was a different encounter? How could we apply the principles of a massage or anything else you allow yourself to indulge in—a custard-filled donut glazed with chocolate comes to mind—to a little dancing in the sheets?

Now we're on the same dance floor. Wink, wink. This is how we need to approach our time with our husbands. Be present. Indulge fully. Enjoy every last sensation.

Be present.

I know during those "special times" we as women can be

somewhere else in our minds. We could be thinking about our grocery lists, or a new outfit we'd like, or the breakfast tacos we ate the morning before, or (you fill in the blank). Learn to train yourself to be present—mind, body, and soul. Do everything you can to stay focused and attentive to the present activities.

How?

There is much we can learn from a visit to the spa. Think about ways you can apply these pamper day points to your love life (or future love life), physically and mentally. Your mental state will be a huge factor in the kind of experience you have with your husband when that moment arrives. Correction: *moments*. Many, many moments.

Take all of these principles and apply each one. Laura began her day with a mind-set of anticipation, expectation, and gratification. This, my dear loved one, is how to approach your physical adventures with your husband—with anticipation, expectation, and gratification. Every day. And twice on Saturday. I'm giving you a shy smirk.

Back to my original point: take your time and relax. If you are tense, it will not go well. If you do feel tense or can't seem to relax, then tell him. Ask him to slow down if you need him to. Like Mama said when you were two, "Use your words." It's okay to mix words and sex. If you want to. Or not. It's up to you. Craft your own love den.

Enjoy Him

On that love-note, here's another verse to ponder: "The wife does not have authority over her own body, but the husband does; and likewise also the husband does not have authority over his own body, but the wife does" (1 Corinthians 7:4).

In other words, enjoy him. Remember when you were little and got your first Easy-Bake Oven or Cabbage Patch doll and you were so excited to play with your new toy? Ahem. New toy. All yours to enjoy.

God tells us throughout the Bible to fully indulge in our physical relationships with our husbands. It's His will for you to enjoy this part of your married life. It's a big shift from *No!* to *Go!*, but always remember the *Go!* is a gift from God. Your husband is a gift from God. Revel in this gift.

SECRET SEX MISSION #2

This is your mission if you wish to accept it: Read through the Song of Solomon. Think about or, even better, write out your expectations with regard to your first sexual experience with your husband. Spend some time praying about it. Decide to make sex an area you will always be open to communicate about and work on, loving him with all you've got. If you're already married, reminisce back to your first sexual experience with your husband. Think through areas that have improved and areas you'd like to "go back to."

ASK HIM

Be bold and inquire what expectations your husband has for your first night. How close are you both to being on the "same bed"? If you're already married, take a stroll back to those first few weeks together and what your playtime looked like. Are there "games" he'd like to revisit?

CHAPTER 3

SEX AND YOUR MIND

> NOT TONIGHT, HONEY—
> MY FAVORITE TV SERIES JUST GOT CANCELED.

The surgery was rougher than we had anticipated. After almost a week, I was released from the hospital and finally in my own bed. My darling husband stayed with me. He watched television as I laid my head on his chest and slept for hours.

Home. Safe. Secure.

It is one of my sweetest memories. I think on it often.

What does this have to do with sex? you wonder. Everything. You can either choose to think about sweet memories or choose to disregard them. Remembering endearing moments and occasions like this can majorly enhance your desire for your husband.

The mind is our biggest sex organ. We can use it to the fullest; the key is using thoughts to enrich desire. If we choose to. We can learn to control our thoughts and harness this very powerful tool.

We've all heard the statistics about how often men think about sex. For fun, give your husband a clicker for a day and ask him to click every time he thinks about sex. The next day, you take the clicker and do the same. It will make for fun conversation. The naked truth is, for many women, contemplating how to bake a moister birthday cake or planning the next vacation would trump thoughts of sex. Herein lies our dilemma.

We can train our minds to zoom in more on sexual musings.

We can ramp up sexy thoughts in our brains to help us ramp

up sexy time in the bedroom. Most professional athletes "see" themselves performing at their peak in their off time. Granted, maybe that's not exactly the same, but are you tracking with me a little?

I'm talking about the "sport" of focusing on your husband and loving him. God repeatedly commands us to love our husbands both emotionally *and* physically, and He wants us to have a healthy, happy marriage—emotionally *and* physically. Did you read the Song of Solomon as suggested in chapter 2? That's not a book you'd want to read with your grandma.

If you're anything like me, there are days when bedroom rodeo is the last sport you want to play. Why? Because I feel like I can't stand him, let alone want to be near him. Usually because my feelings have been hurt. Girlfriend—*snap snap*—can you relate? At times like these we need to take the reins and steer our minds in a more productive direction. As women, we can sometimes allow our feelings to rule the day. I've allowed my mind to take me on detours—stopping at "What if. . . ?" "I should have. . . ," and "I hate my life!"—and then had to claw my way back to happily-ever-after again. Sometimes it takes a stop at "Honey, can we talk?" so I can work through my hurts and sort through my negative emotions.

Here's a tip to stay off Misery Island: on days you don't feel madly in love, you need to slow your roll and strangle your circumstances. Stop and ask, If I felt wildly in love, how would I *act*? And then do whatever that is. Recognize that feelings can lie to you. Love is not always a *feeling*. Love is a commitment. Love is an action word. Love is a choice. Let's take a better detour to "Love is patient, love is kind and is not jealous; love does not brag and is not arrogant, does not act unbecomingly; it does not seek its own, is not provoked, does not take into account a wrong suffered" (1 Corinthians 13:4–5). At how many weddings have you heard those verses read? Those are some mighty powerful instructions from God. Don't allow your emotions to take charge. Once you start "acting" in loving ways, your feelings will follow.

Let's pause here to clarify a few things. Please do not misunderstand what I'm saying here. I am not saying you are to be a bath mat for your spouse or allow yourself to be treated poorly. That is not love. Permitting someone to manipulate or mistreat you is not an act of love. This would not be good for you, for him, and especially for your marriage. We must draw a line at abuse and seek whatever help we need to get back to good health in our marriages.

In every marriage there are comments that can inadvertently hurt, mistakes that can grieve our hearts, and actions that can be misunderstood, triggering negative emotions—all accidents. No one is purposefully trying to hurt the other. This kind of stuff is the day-to-day of marriage, and we need to be on guard against letting our emotions push us into a sea of "poor me," an attitude that will only cause great harm to our emotional health and to our marital union and marital bed.

Controlling what you allow yourself to meditate on will have a huge effect on your feelings and also have huge implications for how you will love your husband both inside and outside of the bedroom. Your mind is your most powerful tool for keeping things steamy in the passion department.

Are You Ready?

Think of setting your mind on sex like you would set the dial on your washing machine. Normal wash. Quick wash. Permanent press. Heavy duty. Delicates. Set your mind to *Expect*; then you won't be "rinsed off" when he wants to "wash the clothes." Eat breakfast, brush your teeth, turn on your car, turn on your husband. It's just part of your day.

One day after my husband came home from work, I was preparing dinner in the kitchen. I had a knife in one hand and a tomato in the other. He randomly said, "Do you want to go in the bedroom?"

What did you do? Throw the tomato at him?

Uh, no. I did pause, though. And took a quick inventory. *Where is my son? That's right, in his room working on homework. My daughter? Not home yet. Dinner? Anything burning or need to go in the fridge? Nope. Put down the knife. All clear.*

Then I asked, "Really?" just to clarify. My husband can be a bit of a practical joker, and I didn't want to embarrass myself by assuming I have rad chopping skills.

He said, "Yup."

And we washed some clothes before dinner.

If this sounds off or odd to you, let's look at it from a different angle. Consider the alternative. I could have turned down his offer without any backlash. My night still would have been okay. Eat dinner. Clean up the dishes. Blah, blah, blah. But instead, blah, blah, blah turned into va-va-voom. The *entire* night was amazing. The air of happiness permeated the house—everyone was happy. Family dinner was better than usual, and oh, guess who did the dishes that night? Not me! Which would you rather have? Okay, or amazing? When you look at it from this angle, it really is an easy choice.

It's all in the state of mind. Think of a diver on the edge of a diving board prepared to jump and anticipating slicing through the water. Keep your mind primed, like a diver ready to jump. I make a point daily to think about my husband in a positive way and in a passionate way. Sex is an important part of marriage, and we need to plan for it like we would grocery shopping or picking up the kids from school.

But what if you're on the diving board and the whistle doesn't blow?

Easy—then jump in first. In other words, if you're ready to go and he's not, then you start things up. Either way, it's a win-win. Don't be timid about being the initiator for "taking the magic bus to Manchester." Men love that.

Now it's time to unpack how to be that diver ready to jump. Please consider the following tried-and-true steps for making sweaty yoga a normal part of your mind-set.

Prayer Power

Pray. Sound a bit trite to you? Give it a try and see what happens. Prayer is the easiest step, *and* the most powerful. What does the perfect sex life look like to you? If your answer is *none*, then you need to start there and ask God for a change of heart.

What is it you want in this area of your life? Be specific and ask God for all your heart's desires. Pray and then expect that God will answer.

On days your husband is giving you those signals but you don't feel operational, send up an SOS (Start Operation System) prayer. Something like this: "Lord, You know the last thing I want to do today is roll around with him. Can You change my heart?" When you pray, and also pray specifically for *him* every day, it can make a world of difference in your heart and in the sheets.

Some mornings I wake up before my husband. Instead of getting up, I stay in bed, and as we're snuggling I pray for him until he opens his eyes. This starts my day with a loving and positive attitude toward him.

Pray for your husband, and not just in the morning but throughout the day as well. Every time you trip over his shoes, pray, "Thank You, God, for a man with big feet." Every time he leaves whiskers in the sink, pray, "Thank You, God, that I have a man in the house." Every time you hear him snore, pray, "Thank You, God, for a man who is still breathing."

I know snoring is annoying. But any widow could give you food for thought about snoring. If he's snoring, he's breathing, which means you get another day with him.

One of the most beautiful prayers I've ever read was written by Elisabeth Elliot in her book *Love Has a Price Tag*: "The garbage truck grinds up the hill outside my window (for this house is on a hill). And there is the sound of someone breathing—beside me. Lord, Father of Spirits, Lover of Souls, my Light and my Stronghold, thanks! Thanks for the greatest of earthly blessings, marriage. My prayer goes on for a little while—thanksgiving and petition (that I may be the sort of wife I ought to be, that together we may accomplish the will of the Father)."[1]

If you don't know the story of Elisabeth Elliot, her first husband, Jim Elliot, was killed while he was on a mission trip to Ecuador, and her second husband died of cancer. She wrote the above while married to her third husband. We can learn much from her about appreciating the husband with whom God has blessed us.

Maybe you are struggling and feel as though you have tried everything. Prayer always works. Start with a prayer of thanksgiving through an attitude of praise and appreciation.

At one time my husband played in a softball league. He loved playing and he loved hanging out with the guys. Invariably he would leave his heavy softball bag in the middle of the kitchen the next morning. Now, I knew he didn't leave it there on purpose; he came home tired and had merely forgotten about it. Nevertheless, the very sight of that bag irritated me. I hated dragging it to the garage. Why couldn't he do it?

One day while dragging the bag and grumbling under my breath, I decided to switch out the moaning for prayer. I prayed for him all the way into the garage. "God, thank You for a man who has the ability to play softball. . . ." Every time I saw that stinkin' bag, I prayed for him. It wasn't long before the sight of the bag didn't irritate me anymore. Grumblings turned into endearments and warm feelings, altering my mood from wanting to slug him to wanting to kiss him.

What if every time you had a negative thought about your husband you transformed it into a prayer of praise and thanksgiving?

How different would your marriage be if every time you saw something about your husband that irritated you, instead of giving in to the irritation, you prayed a prayer of gratitude?

How different would your evenings be if instead of becoming aggravated with your husband, you thanked God for him?

Thought Management

Listen to the words of the great theologian Rocky Balboa: "I never asked you to stop bein' a woman, you know? Please, I'm askin' you, please. . .don't ask me to stop bein' a man. Please."[2]

On that quote, let's move on to the commode. We expect our men to always put the seat down, and if they don't, we can become incensed. We think we get to set the bar—or seat—on this. I get it: it's not fun falling in! I'm bringing up this silly subject to make a point to be careful what you allow to float around in your head. If annoyances are flying, fun isn't. If you get annoyed at "the seat" and carry a grudge against him throughout the day, how do you think this will play out in your fun zone?

(If he ever puts the seat down, thank him profusely for it. I'll bet it won't take long before he's putting it down on a regular basis. He may even clean it from time to time.)

Don't get bothered with your man for doing things *men do*. Remember, he's a man. He will think like a man and act like a man. This doesn't mean we don't ask for what we desire from our husbands. Married people make requests of each other. Go ahead and ask for what you want; just don't demand. Like Dr. Gary Chapman says in his book *The Five Love Languages*, request what your wants are; do not demand.[3] When we demand, we're basically treating our spouses like children.

Anytime I make a request of my husband and he doesn't get to it on my timetable—which is quite often very different from his—I refuse to let *waiting* come between us. Whatever the circumstance, you *can* make the choice not to be irritated. Always remember that love doesn't demand. That's just rude.

Sex for a woman is so much more than the physical act—we desire to feel loved and cherished. For most of us, if we don't feel loved and cherished, the thought of getting close is downright repulsive. That's why we need to keep a pulse on the health of our relationships. In his book *Crazy Good Sex*, Dr. Les Parrott says that even if a man is not feeling particularly close to his wife, it's unlikely he would turn down sex. The same is not true for women. Women need to feel connected emotionally before bonding physically. No emotional connection, no physical connection.[4]

Hence, I dub thee the physical connection police. Since the feeling of being close, connected, and united is what unlocks our passion—our physical desire comes from an emotional desire—to get "cozy" on a regular basis, we need to safeguard our feelings of connectedness.

As women, we tend to have a built-in radar for spotting problems with our relationships. How many times have you gone to your husband with, "Honey, I think we have a problem"? Nine times out of ten, his reply will be something like: "We do? I thought we were fine."

Our husbands are not lying; they really think everything is fine. Most men don't have the same relationship radar that God gave us women. We instinctively know how to be in relationships. This starts very young. Watch children at play, for instance: the little girls will be paired up, sometimes not even playing but talking instead. How often do you see two little boys sitting down and talking over a cup of hot cocoa?

We women have a gift. Use this radar to keep the love link strong and steamy! Be willing to have those uncomfortable yet necessary conversations when you know tackling an issue will bring deeper intimacy.

Having said that, I am not encouraging you to make an issue out of every little thing. That would be exhausting! There is a difference between occasional blips on the relationship radar and *blipppppppp*. Take time to consider, pray about, and discern what issues need to be surfaced. Then approach him with gentleness and with an understanding attitude, coupled with the goal of improving your marriage.

Identify any triggers that are hindering your desire for sexual intimacy. If you're not feeling like baking the potato, ask yourself, Why? Negative triggers allowed to have top billing can really take the bang out of your love.

An Attitude of Appreciation

Joyce called our church for help with her marriage. She specifically indicated she did not want to talk with a man. My phone rang. It was my husband asking me if I would talk with Joyce. Knowing I'd be driving to LAX later that day and would be in traffic, I scheduled to call her in the afternoon. She was kind and grateful, thanking me profusely for taking time to talk with her. I asked her to tell me what was going on in her relationship and what she needed help with. I listened and listened to numerous grievances Joyce had against her husband—I mean, I had about a two-hour ride, why not give her time to get it all out? She also told me about previous conversations she'd had with numerous pastors at our church, relaying the advice she'd been given and how she didn't agree. I was in a bit of a quandary because I agreed with the pastors' counsel. I knew I needed to tread lightly in order to get through to her and help her. I arrived near LAX and pulled into a parking lot to finish talking with her. I prayed a quick prayer silently and asked God to give me wisdom for how to help her.

I hesitantly proceeded. "Joyce, I understand how you could feel as you do, and I'm sorry for what you're going through, but can I ask you a question?"

She said, "Yes."

"How is your sex life?" I asked.

"Oh, we don't have sex," Joyce answered. "I had a complication after the birth of our daughter, and it's painful for me."

"Is it something you can get fixed?" I inquired.

"Yes," she said.

I continued, "Joyce, can you understand how this could be a bit frustrating for your husband?"

"Well, yes," Joyce replied.

"Can I ask you another question?"

"Yes," she replied willingly.

"Can you tell me something good about your husband?"

"He's a good man and he's never cheated on me," Joyce answered.

"Anything else?" I asked.

"He works hard," she said.

"Anything else?"

"He's a really good dad."

"Okay," I said. "So he's a good man, he's never cheated on you, he works hard, and he's a good dad." Next I asked, "Does he go to church with you?"

"Yes," she said emphatically, "and he's in a home group."

"So"—I took a deep breath—"he's a good man who goes to

church with you. Joyce, do you think maybe he misses being intimate with you and maybe he feels frustrated?" I talked a little about how important the physical relationship is for a man.

I then asked cautiously, "Joyce, do you think you could get this medical issue taken care of?"

"It would cost money," she said.

"How about you tell him you'd like to get it fixed, and see if he thinks it would be money well spent? I'm guessing he'll be happy to cover the expenses."

Suddenly the light came on for Joyce, and she agreed to talk with her husband about seeing a doctor. I prayed for her, and she thanked me. And I thanked God.

The longer we are married, the more we need to look for the magic in the day-to-day. We need to train our minds to maintain an attitude of appreciation. It takes work to appreciate the small things about our husbands and to spot occasions to choose thankfulness. Think on the sweet things they do on a regular basis that we sometimes overlook. Seize every opportunity to mull over acts of kindness.

In preparation for this section, I polled a few happily married friends and asked what they appreciated about their husbands. I expected a few sentences, but what I got back were novels. Here are just a few things these women commended:

- "He works hard."
- "He fixes things."
- "He maintains the cars."
- "He empties the drain in the morning."
- "When he texts me, he starts with, 'Hey sexy!'"
- "He's patient with me."
- "He's a godly man."
- "He holds my hand."

- "He lets cars cut in front of him."
- "He's dependable."

And the praise went on and on.

One friend was adamant about letting me know how cute her husband was. This factor was quite important to her. You would think he was a real hunk. Frankly, I'm not in the habit of rating my friends' husbands on their hunk value, but let me tell you, her husband is. . .how to put this. . .a retired grandpa? I'd never looked at him quite the way she does.

One friend ended with, "I feel like I should be giving you juicier information, but it's just everyday stuff that he does that I appreciate." It's no wonder these ladies put the *happy* in happily married. They look for the magic in the everyday. As you go through your day and come across something your husband has done or said, some kindness or nicety you witnessed or benefited from, praise God for him.

When I had to stop abruptly and my car handled great, I remembered my husband had recently put new tires on my car. *Praise God for him!*

My friend told me her ex-husband used to get mad at her for leaving hair in the shower. Then I realized my husband had been cleaning up my hair for years. *Big praise for him!*

He usually makes our bed in the morning, and as I pass it throughout the day, I say, *Thank You, God, for this amazing man!*

Recently my husband and I were stopped in a pharmacy pick-up line. My wallet was out and my husband was thumbing through it. He pulled out an old picture. It was one of our wedding pictures. . .oh, so many years ago. He looked at the picture, he looked at me. . .and he smiled. He smiled at me again and said, "You look better today than you did on our wedding day." Then he put the picture back in my wallet.

In that moment, I felt all the love he had given me for more than three decades.

It's the magic of the ordinary. I'm willing to bet your husband displays his love for you in countless ways. Don't let those small acts of kindness go unnoticed or unappreciated. Take the time to notice. Pay attention to what's rolling around in your head. What rolls around in there will roll out everywhere else—especially in the way you respond to your hunk.

You Won't Be Able to Keep Your Hands off Him

"Never try to improve your sex life in marriage. Instead, develop honor and security in your relationship and you'll discover how great sex is a by-product of your loving relationship. Build more honor and security, and the sexual satisfaction will naturally increase," write Dr. Gary Smalley and Ted Cunningham in *The Language of Sex*.[5]

When we choose to honor our husbands and look for opportunities to muse over their attractive qualities, positive feelings will flourish. And it goes around and around. Honor yields a natural development of honoring thoughts. Honoring thoughts produce endearing feelings. Endearing feelings generate loving actions. The more respect and honor we have for our husbands, the more we'll want to be close to them.

God designed us for emotional intimacy *and* physical intimacy. Unleash yourself—in your mind and in your body. Tap into your desires. Pay attention to when you feel like "taking Grandma to Applebee's." What causes you to feel like this? It might be memories of past encounters with him, his embrace, his smell, or his tenderness with your children. Once you can identify what creates loving feelings, carefully look for ways to duplicate them.

The more you have sex, the more you'll think about sex, and the more you'll want sex. One begets the other.

What is great sex anyway? Think about that. Do you want to know the answer? Great sex is whatever you decide it is. *You* define the meaning of great sex. You set the standard. You set the bar—no one else! It all starts in your mind. Whatever *you* determine in your mind is great sex *is* great sex. It can be that simple.

Once you key in to these types of thoughts, keep it going. Once you flip that switch, keep it flipped by replaying past encounters over and over in your mind. You can be waiting in line at the post office and improving your marriage at the same time.

Make the choice to stand on the edge of that diving board.

SECRET SEX MISSION #3

This is your mission if you wish to accept it: Strive to think only positive thoughts about your husband for a week, focusing on what you appreciate most about him. Add on sexual thoughts the next week, running your last pleasant sexual encounter through your mind like a rerun over and over. See if this doesn't send your marriage to a new planet—a universe only God can take it to.

ASK HIM

Have a conversation with your husband about what you both consider great sex. Talk about some of your fondest memories. What causes you to feel most fulfilled?

PART 2

HINDRANCES

CHAPTER 4

INTIMACY INTERRUPTED

> NOT TONIGHT, HONEY—
> THE KIDS DEMOLISHSED ME TODAY

Come with me, I've saved you a seat. . .
  Open curtains. Scene 1.

Hannah loved her husband, Steve. She sincerely wanted to please him. She never wanted to say anything that would hurt his feelings or cause him to think she wasn't attracted to him. Or worse, that she had lost her desire for sex.

But she *had* lost her desire. She lost it a long time ago. It was so long ago she couldn't even remember the last time she enjoyed having sex with him. As she stirred the breakfast oatmeal, her mind wandered to his words before he left for work.

"Hannah, can you put the kids to bed early tonight? I would really like some time with you." She knew what that meant. He wanted sex. Again.

Hannah told Steve, "Sure. I'll get them down early."

As the oatmeal started to boil over onto the stove, Hannah quickly turned off the burner. *Maybe if I get a nap in today, I'll have the energy to at least act like I'm enjoying myself tonight.*

She sat down on the floor in her kitchen as every bit of motivation fizzled out of her. The project of cleaning up all the oatmeal on the stove felt overwhelming. Then, toddling into the kitchen, her two-year-old son, Zach, sat his little bottom right in her lap. "Breafest, Mommy?" Zach gave her reason to get up and get moving again, helping her remember why she loved being a mom.

"Well, yes, my little prince, Mommy has it ready right now." She gave him a kiss and a hug, then picked him up and placed him in his high chair. Katie, her three-year-old, came running out of her bedroom wearing her pink tutu and sat expectantly at the breakfast table.

"Is the ballerina ready for oatmeal?"

"Yes, Mommy. I was dancing in my room and got extra hungry. I did five spins."

Hannah served the oatmeal and went on with the rest of her day like a robot. Kitchen cleanup, reading time, playtime, nap time. She tried to nap too, but Katie begged her to watch *Sesame Street* again. Hannah couldn't resist her big blue eyes.

"Mommy, can we eat crackers again, please, and watch it together?"

As they watched, Zach climbed into Hannah's lap.

I love my kids. I love my husband. What is wrong with me? I don't have desire for anything anymore. I feel numb.

The rest of the day went on as usual with Hannah in a robotic state. Afternoon cleanup, dinner preparation, Steve's arrival home, dinnertime, baths for the kids, devotions, kids tucked in early, and. . .now to the bedroom.

She forced herself to smile as he glanced at her from across the room.

"I'd really like to keep the lights on," Steve said.

"Okay. Great." Hannah had always wondered what it might be like with candles, but she wanted to make Steve happy, and he liked the lights on. She didn't understand why.

As she climbed into bed, the smell of garlic and onions on his breath from his favorite lunchtime sandwich repulsed her. Steve loved garlic and onions, and she would never say anything to him about not liking the smell; she didn't want to hurt his feelings.

He held her tight. But it was a little too tight. Steve didn't realize the strength of his arms. She felt as if she couldn't breathe. He never seemed to touch her where she wanted, and sometimes he unknowingly hurt her—but she never told him. How could she potentially make him feel bad? She loved him and wanted to please him.

After being intimate, Steve kissed her and told her he loved her. Hannah told him back, then went into the bathroom. As she returned to the bed, she noticed he had already dozed off. She slipped in beside him, facing the opposite way, as tears rolled down her face.

Why do I always feel so sad after?

She mustn't tell Steve. She loved him. She respected him. He was a good man. She would never hurt him.

We're going to deviate from our narrative briefly. Consider this an intermission.

Usually on my husband's day off, we spend time together. On one of these days he wasn't his usual self. I could tell he needed some time to himself and left him alone for most of the day. Talking was scarce. At the end of the day, he said, "Thank you for leaving me alone." A funny thing to be thanked for, but I was happy to get appreciation. It wasn't easy for me because I like to talk.

Men oftentimes like to hibernate. Most women like to talk. And talk and talk. But when it comes to the subject of sex, we tend to clam up. Why is that? Talking about sex is just as important as other household and relational topics.

Intermission over. Open the curtains for scene 2.

One day Hannah was given a book titled *The Intimacy You Crave: Straight Talk about Sex and Pancakes*. She never would have bought such a book for herself, but a dear friend had purchased it for her, and she decided to read it. At first Hannah was shocked by its contents. At the urging of her friend, she kept reading.

After finishing the book, Hannah knew she needed to talk with Steve. Every day she prayed for the courage to broach the subject. How would she even begin? One day passed, two days, and then a week went by. She kept praying for an opportunity.

And then it happened—a window of opportunity opened. Hannah was flipping pancakes on the kitchen stove when Steve came up behind her and put his arms around her. Knowing he couldn't see her face, she blurted out, "Can we talk about sex tonight?"

"What?" Steve asked.

She thought to herself, *Oh Steve, don't make me ask again*, but said nothing.

Steve turned her around so he could look into her eyes.

"You want to talk about sex?"

Hannah took a deep breath. "Yes."

"Okay. I'll see you after work."

Steve kissed her and went out the door.

Hannah collapsed to the floor.

What just happened? That was pretty easy. Thank You, God.

Zach ran in and sat on her lap. "Hi, Mommy, breafest?"

High chair, breakfast, cleanup, story time, nap time, a trip to the park. The day seemed to be creeping by slowly. And then from the kitchen window she saw Steve's car pull into the driveway. He was home early. She hadn't even started dinner yet. Hannah decided to go outside and greet Steve. He seemed happier than usual.

As they came into the house, the kids ran up to greet him.

Then Steve said these magic words: "Kids, Daddy is going to put on a movie for you while he helps Mommy make dinner." Steve came into the kitchen and washed his hands. Looking at Hannah with hands raised, he said, "Okay, I'm all yours. How can I help?"

Hannah had forgotten how fun it could be to work in the kitchen together. It reminded her of when they were first married, and it felt like a fairy tale.

Steve didn't mention anything about Hannah's request that morning. She was deep in thought, wondering, *Did he forget? Should I ask again? No, I'm not asking again. Once is enough. Maybe he doesn't want to talk about it and he's trying to be extra nice so I don't bring it up again.*

They all ate dinner together as a family. Hannah felt anxious throughout the meal, wondering if Steve had forgotten about her request that morning. Or even worse, if he *hadn't* forgotten and she would have to follow up on her request and talk about— *gulp*—sex. She had played what she would say over and over in her head, but could she really say those things?

Dinner was over, and Steve began to clean up the dinner dishes.

What? Who is this guy? she mused.

As soon as the kitchen was cleaned, he scooped Zach into his arms and headed for the bathtub. She could hear the sound of Zach laughing as his daddy played boats with him.

After Zach was ready for bed, Steve then gave Katie a bath and got her ready for bed. Hannah could hear Katie say, "Daddy, I want to wear my mermaid pajamas."

"Okay, my little princess, and then Daddy will comb your hair."

Once both of the kids were ready for bed, Hannah could hear Steve doing devotions with them in Zach's room. Suddenly Hannah didn't just want to talk about sex; she wanted to *have* sex!

Maybe I should just go into the bedroom and put on that little nightie I've never worn.

Just as she was about to head to the bedroom, Steve walked into the living room.

"Okay. Kids all bathed and tucked in for bed. Let's talk about sex."

Hannah was stunned. *He did remember!*

She took a deep breath as they sat on the couch together. Steve looked at her and didn't say a word.

Slightly terrified, she dove in. "Steve, I love you and really want to make you happy. I know I haven't been overly responsive to you in the bedroom. Maybe if we could talk about it, I'd be able to get into things more."

Steve nodded.

"I was wondering if maybe we could put some candles in our bedroom and light them the next time?"

Steve nodded and said, "Great idea."

"And I know you love those gyro sandwiches at your favorite spot, but you come home smelling like garlic and onions."

"And you don't like that smell," Steve said.

"Correct," Hannah confirmed.

Steve quickly said, "I'm pretty sick of that place. I've been wanting to start changing up lunch anyway."

"Steve, you're so strong, and I love that, but sometimes you hold me so tight, I feel like I can't breathe. Sometimes it's a little too tight."

"I can be gentler. Just let me know next time."

"And there are. . .well. . .things that I'd like you to try. Simple things like touching me in different areas besides, well. . .you know."

"My hands are all yours! Anything else?"

"Well, just one more thing. Do you think we can cuddle after? I'd really like that. Sometimes I feel extra emotional after, and I need you to just hold me for a few minutes before we fall asleep."

"Done," he said without hesitation.

Hannah fell into his arms. She kissed him. That night they never made it to the bedroom where Steve was going to light some candles. . . .

The next day Steve left the house with a big smile. And Hannah found herself smiling too.

After that night they continued to talk about their sex life on a regular basis. Hannah completed the book and did all of the Secret Sex Missions at the close of each chapter. She never realized how much better her life could be with a few strategic adjustments.

Close curtains. Important note: not all husbands will respond the way Steve did. Talking about sex may be uncomfortable for your husband, and he might even make jokes about it in an attempt to hide his uneasiness. Or he may need time to process what you've said to him. Be willing to give him time, and then revisit the subject when he's ready. Don't be offended if at first he doesn't seem to take you seriously and either jokes or clams up. It's possible he just doesn't know how to deal with what you're saying in the moment. Be patient but don't give up.

Is anything blocking your love life? Maybe it's time to take back control. Let's examine some hindrances that may be slowing down your fun.

Top Ten Hindrances to Intimacy

Although fictional, Hannah's struggle is not unique. We each need to tackle any and all hindrances to sexual intimacy, whether in our minds or otherwise. Be willing to wrestle with the following hindrances—like a feisty fox terrier—and allow God to chisel His masterpiece, ushering in a more fulfilling union.

1. Body Image

After my kids were born, I gained a significant amount of weight. How much? Well. . .ahem. . .like fifty pounds. Okay, okay. Seventy. Yes, seventy pounds, as in seven-zero. It was rough. But you know what I learned? The weight gain didn't slow down my husband's desire or impede his fun. Maybe your husband isn't as gracious in this area, but—his response aside for now—we each need to eradicate our body issues by attacking them head-on.

Many of us carry around a poor body image that keeps us from enjoying our husbands to the fullest—*because of the way we feel about our own bodies.* Body issues can become a barrier to sexual expression. . .if you allow them to. This barrier is so common to so many women that I've devoted a whole chapter to this subject; we'll tackle it together in chapter 5.

2. Sexual Abuse

I hate that I have to write about this. I hate that some of us have to deal with it. Sadly, as too many of us know, sexual abuse is a tool of Satan attempting to bring down a family years before a woman even says, "I do." Our mighty God and Savior is greater and stronger than any evil force. We *can* experience healing and freedom from sexual abuse. As with body image, there is much more to this issue than can be said here, so we'll cover it in depth in chapter 6.

For now let's address some of the sneakier hindrances that can lead you away from harmonious matrimonial polka. Are you with me, sister?

3. Anger

When I'm angry, my desire for sex plummets to zilch. Can you relate? Anger, bitterness, and resentment are so very destructive. They can ruin your marriage and certainly your sex life.

My dear and godly friend Alice Zellmer—who's in her eighties! —paraphrases Ephesians 4:26 this way: "Don't let the sun go down upon your wrath; it will ruin your sex life." Words of wisdom right there.

If you find yourself feeling angry often, please get to the bottom of the cause and don't allow anger and bitterness to destroy your marriage. Take it to the Lord and ask Him to help you.

4. Unforgiveness

Marriage is a ministry of forgiveness. If you are married for any length of time, you'll soon find that you need to become proficient at forgiving. Holding on to resentment will invariably block your libido.

The easiest way for me to prevent an unforgiving heart is to remember the many times my husband has forgiven me, and especially the many times my Lord has forgiven me. *Way* too many to count. If you do want to keep score, tally how many times your husband has forgiven you, and not the other way around.

On one occasion, I had spent the day fasting and praying and, in the midst of that, became aware I needed to go to my husband and ask forgiveness. Becoming painfully aware of how I had spilled my rotten attitude on him, I knew I needed to apologize. I waited until the following day while we were out to dinner *alone*. I told him what God had showed me. As I apologized, I began to cry. Before I could finish, he pulled me in close and held me. He forgave me instantly.

Never am I more attracted to my husband than when he shows me forgiveness. In turn, a forgiving wife is extremely appealing to a husband. (Nudity helps too.)

Think about that. The amount of forgiveness we desire is the same amount we need to extend. I don't know about you, but I am a mess and need forgiveness often. Forgiveness serves as a strong anchor for any secure and healthy marriage. We are all in process and need understanding and forgiveness.

When your husband makes a mistake, forgive him and don't hold it against him. He'll love you for it and will probably show his appreciation in some way. Dr. John Gray writes about this in his book *Venus on Fire, Mars on Ice*, saying, "Men take notice when we overlook a mistake and even if he doesn't say a word, he noticed it. Guaranteed."[1]

Hurt feelings are a hazard of marriage. Don't keep an account of wrongs suffered. Make the decision ahead of time to always choose forgiveness.

5. Boredom
Sex is boring; he always does the same old thing the same old way.
Wah-wah. . .

While at the gym one morning, I noticed a lady on a cardio machine in front of me. I thought to myself, *Boy, she is always here at the same time, doing the same thing on the same machine. She's in a rut!* Then it hit me. I was *behind* her at the same time, doing the same thing on the same machine.

If sex is boring for you and you feel like you're in a rut, then change you, and in doing so you'll change the whole "moving furniture" equation. In *The Language of Sex*, Dr. Gary Smalley and Ted Cunningham report, "The top thing a woman wants from a man is *gentleness*. The top thing a man wants from a woman is *responsiveness*. Just as a woman craves gentleness, a man desires that the woman respond to him."[2]

Respond to him differently and you'll change everything. One time I bought purple silk sheets and put them on our bed. That night as my husband got into bed, his pillow went flying across the room. Not exactly what I had anticipated. It wasn't very romantic, but it made for a good laugh. And it definitely changed things up! Often during the night when my husband or I rolled over, our pillows would shoot out like missiles. It wasn't long before we changed back to our regular sheets, but it was fun for a while. Even if things don't go as planned, you can still have fun, even if not in an erotic way. Fun leads to more *fun*.

Here are a few ideas to get you thinking.

- Pamper yourself and get really dressed up just for him— and for *fun*.
- Buy some sexy lingerie or put on a fashion show with the lingerie you already have.
- Put together a playlist of songs that help you feel romantic, and play it all day and that night.
- If your budget allows, make reservations for a night in a hotel room and let him know what's on the agenda.
- Tell him you're going to take over and for him to stay still until you say he can move.
- Write out a list of "activities" you'd like to try and slip it to him or write it on the bathroom mirror in lipstick.
- Wake him up with "adventurous" touching, or jump in the shower with him when he isn't expecting it.
- Change locations and consider a room other than your bedroom.
- Buy colored lightbulbs or string Christmas lights in your bedroom.
- If you have kids, send them to Grandma's house for the night and then have a contest for who can be the loudest.
- Purchase a set of satin sheets. Or silk sheets if you're brave enough. Ha-ha.
- Buy some body lotion or oil and take turns giving each other a massage.
- Take a bubble bath and open a bottle of sparkling cider.

- Upgrade those tattered panties to something sexier.

6. Negative Talk and Thoughts

Negative talk and thoughts are deadly to any relationship. Don't talk negatively about your husband or indulge those who do. Negative talk creates negative opinions; negative opinions create negative emotions; negative emotions lead to no sex; and no sex can lead to a not-so-exciting marriage.

As we talked about in chapter 3, pay attention to the thoughts floating around in your head; allowing even the smallest irritation to linger can cause you to feel really irked with him. When a negative thought pops up, like *I'm so mad he has to work late again; he doesn't care about me!* try reframing it to something like this: *I love my husband's work ethic; he works so hard for our family.* Resist any negative thoughts about your husband. Recall sweet words he has said to you, a time he forgave you, a time he stopped by the store for you, or a time he didn't get upset *or* complain when you took out the fender on his beloved pickup truck with detailed graphics running from the front tires to the back that he spent countless hours getting just the way he liked . . . . Big sigh. I can't be the only one who's done this, can I?

Exchange negative thoughts for positive ones and find something about your husband for which you are grateful; start a list and read through it every time you find yourself stuck in a negative thought pattern.

7. Exhaustion

We have all felt exhausted from time to time. I wish I could offer a simple answer for this one, but anything I might say in this area would probably sound trite. I will tell you that I have been there. Many times I've had to beg God for enough energy just to get through the day.

Setting priorities is the key. What will we choose to do with the energy we do have? Sex needs to be high on the priority scale, yet we often place other less important endeavors before it. Give sex a bit of a bump on your scale.

Having said this, I understand you may be in a season of battling for your health or caring for small children. Bringing an infant home can lessen your desire to do much else besides caring for your baby. I once had a season of nursing a newborn and chasing a toddler at the same time. After having little hands grab at me all day long, the last thing I looked forward to was having man-hands grab at me at night.

Talk with your husband about how you're feeling and come up with creative ideas together to keep each other a priority. Consider taking long showers together, sleeping in one day a week when he takes care of the kids so you can be rested for nighttime activities, finding times in your week to fit in a quick "joust," streamlining tasks to create more breaks, or idling back on other commitments outside of your home. When I was in the season of raising small children, I scheduled in my husband, that is, I let him know when the "hot date" was. Before I make myself sound better than I was, here's what that looked like sometimes: "Okay, I've got thirty minutes right now; after that your window is closed." Not the sexiest way to initiate, I suppose—not that I got any complaints—but communicating what times and situations work best for both of you is important.

If you are exhausted—especially too exhausted for "buying Frisbees"—do something about it. It may be as simple as taking some downtime. Schedule breaks regularly. We all need time to rest and recuperate; take time to do so. Or if making some changes doesn't seem to help, you may need to see a doctor to get your hormones or thyroid checked or to rule out other health problems. In any case, don't stand back and let exhaustion damage your marriage. And then go buy those Frisbees! (Again, if that didn't make sense, please read the introductory section "Read This First.")

8. Too Much Focus on Work or Kids

Alrighty, now we're talkin'! I know all too well what it's like to get wrapped up in work or kids. As a mom, I naturally tend to get caught up in the lives of one or all of my children. As my kids were growing, I had to remind myself often—too often, in fact—that eventually they would leave, but my hubby was here to stay. Consequently, I needed to put him first. Not only was this best for my marriage; it was best for my kids as well. Most likely our children will be married for a longer duration of time than they will be living in our homes. One of the best gifts we can send them off with is a model of a loving home where Mom and Dad loved each other fully and made each other a priority.

If your children ended up in a marriage like yours, would you be proud or terrified? Consider this: every day, you are teaching them what a marriage looks like.

As I write this, two of my children are now married. If you take away nothing else from this section, please hear this: I am immeasurably thankful, as difficult as it was, that I put my husband first through the "kid years." I see my adult children loving their spouses all out and making them a priority. There are few greater rewards as a parent.

We can also become so focused on our careers that we lose focus on our marriages. Finding balance is difficult but is worth the struggle. Please don't let anything temporary weaken what's eternal.

9. Something He's Doing or Not Doing

Years ago my husband decided to let his hair grow long. But he didn't just let it grow long. *He had a mullet!* I personally have nothing against men with long hair, but in terms of starting my engine, a mullet doesn't push the accelerator.

The longer his hair got, the more he liked it—and the more I disliked it. Worse yet, it was like he was in a special club. Other guys with long hair—total strangers—would single him out. As if they had a secret society. Suddenly he was in this special club, and he reveled in it. I recall one guy praising him and saying, "Hey! Fellow long hair!"

Someone, please help me. I hated the hair.

This long hair phase persisted for about seven months. All the while, I remained silent and held in my massive displeasure. He seemed to love it so much, I just couldn't bring myself to tell him I hated it.

I was in a quandary. I didn't want him to withdraw his membership in the cool club, but on the other hand, I didn't want to have sex with him either. Every time I hugged or kissed him, I got hair in my face. Every time I rolled over in bed, I fell into a swamp of hair. I still cringe when I think back on *that mullet*. Conflicted, I kept telling myself that I could get over this feeling and work through it. I. Was. Wrong.

One day Mike asked me for one of my ponytail holders. If there was anything worse than a mullet plastered to the back of the head of the man I loved, it was sharing my ponytail holders with that thing. That did it for me. I knew it was time to say something or I was going to burst.

I calmly sat my husband down and apologized profusely as I explained my dilemma. He took it surprisingly well.

The next day he got a haircut! Bye-bye, mullet, bye-bye. Never to return. *Thank You, God!*

If there is something your husband is doing or not doing that is deterring you from wanting to open the gates of Mordor—and you've sincerely tried to work through it but cannot—then it's time to have a talk with him. Perhaps your husband needs to work on his hygiene, or maybe he unknowingly treats you harshly and this causes you to shy away from intimacy. That's understandable. Lovingly confront the issue. Maybe your relationship needs some mending. It can start with you, first by loving him unconditionally, and second by loving him enough to address the issues that are holding you back.

Be very careful *how* you say what you need to say, and *when* you say what you need to say. Be respectful and kind in your delivery. You will find in Esther 5:4, 7 and 7:2 that Queen Esther prepared an elaborate banquet for the king not once but twice before she made her request of him. Follow that respectful example as you proceed.

10. Unmet Expectations

Expectations. When the gap between what you think he *should* be doing and reality becomes a nagging irritation, you may have a problem with unmet expectations. Is he currently meeting all your expectations? Yeah, I didn't think so. When I set expectations, I am disappointed too.

Maybe *he* doesn't need to close the gap; maybe *you* need to reframe the gap. Are you ready to reframe the gap? Are you ready for the key to being satisfied in your marriage? I have the secret equation for contentment in your marriage. This is revolutionary.

Zero expectations.

You read that right. Zero expectations! Did I get your attention? Okay, okay, let's change it to reasonable expectations. *What's reasonable?* Of course a husband needs to be faithful to his marriage vows and follow through on being the husband he promised to be before God. What I want to emphasize is that if you find yourself using words like "He should be. . . ," "I deserve. . . ," and my favorite, "He should know. . . ," you may be taking your God-honoring and good-willed husband for granted. When you hear in your head chants of *He should be doing this* and *I deserve that*, it's time for a heart check.

You cannot be grateful and disappointed at the same time. Get up every day with a heart filled with gratitude and freedom from resentment. Always choose thankfulness. Let's stop right now and take a few minutes to come up with reasons to be thankful for your husband. Stop where you are right now. See this stop sign? Don't just barrel through it! No California stops, please. Seriously, will you take a break and think of the many things about your husband for which you can be thankful? Write them down.

(Go ahead, I'll wait.)

Make it a habit to stop and add to this list every day. Think back to when you were dating. Maybe he left you love letters or surprised you with special dates or left a rose on your car. Now that you are married, he is doing the equivalent of that by working hard and then coming home. In her book *For Women Only*, author Shaunti Feldhahn interviewed over one thousand men. Her research found that working hard and providing for his family are central features of the way a man is wired, and in essence he is saying, "I love you." His hard work is an expression of his love, dedication, and loyalty.[3]

If you have a man who works hard, *you are a fortunate woman*. Praise God and sing "Hallelujah!" Thank your Father in heaven for that man. If there is something you need to ask your husband for—don't hint at what you desire—ask him directly. That's right, ask for what you want. Don't assume he should know. If you have a man who is faithful to your wedding vows and comes home at the end of the day, chances are you have a good man. Choose thankfulness. And, I might add, if he comes home at the end of the day and feels like buttering the biscuit—he is saying he loves you! Don't allow unmet expectations to become a barrier between you and great sex.

SECRET SEX MISSION #4

This is your mission if you wish to accept it: Begin your day by showing appreciation for your husband and thinking of ways you can bless your man. Concentrate on being thankful for him, and allow your mind to dwell on those grateful thoughts. Then sit down and write out a list of the specific obstacles getting in the way of greater intimacy. Brainstorm ways to eradicate these obstacles. Identify the biggest hindrance and work on it this week.

ASK HIM

What does your husband feel is your biggest obstacle to greater sexual intimacy? If you are open to suggestions, brainstorm some ideas for how to overcome these obstacles together. (Consider reading chapters 5 and 6 together if body image and/or sexual abuse are hindrances for you.)

CHAPTER 5

BUT I HATE MY BODY

> NOT TONIGHT, HONEY—
> I FEEL FAT.

What is the perfect body anyway?
"I don't know, but I know it's not mine!"
—Every female

Emma was over the moon excited and giddy beyond any feelings she had ever experienced before. The school dance was coming up, and she had never been before. Chemistry had been her least favorite subject, but suddenly going to her fourth-period class was the highlight of her day.

Jason sat in front of her and would turn around to talk with her at every opportunity. Emma got lost in his green eyes, sometimes unable to follow what he was saying as she peered into his smiling face. He was hot. As hot as a teenage boy can get. Emma felt pretty and special every time she talked with him. The school dance was three weeks away and she felt confident that this time she'd have a date and finally get asked to dance.

At night before falling asleep, Emma would daydream about going to the dance with Jason. What would she wear? What would he wear? What color would her corsage be? How would he ask her to dance? Maybe the night would end with a kiss?

"You seem rather chipper this morning," Emma's mom commented as she drove her to school. "In fact, you've seemed quite happy all week."

Emma paused. Should she tell her mom about Jason? Emma took a quick breath and said, "Well, the school dance is coming up, and I think this guy in my chemistry class is going to ask me."

"Oh Emma," her mother said with a soft but firm voice, "fat girls don't get asked to dances." Her mom meant well; she just didn't want her daughter to be disappointed, and used this opportunity to nudge her to lose weight.

That day when Jason turned to talk with Emma, instead of responding to him, she looked down. Over time Jason stopped turning around and Emma was not asked to the dance. Mom was right—fat girls don't get asked to dances.

What was the message you received about your body from your parents and peers when you started becoming aware of your sexuality?

I can remember having body-image issues since I was in elementary school. Sister, don't think you are the only one. We all have them. I suppose there are women out there somewhere who totally love their bodies just as they are, but I have never met one. And I've been around a long time, enough to collect plenty of wrinkles. Wrinkles, ugh! Another issue piled on the vanity heap.

My husband has been very encouraging in this area. He's such a prince, often telling me I'm beautiful. Oh, to see myself through his eyes and the Father's eyes. Yeah, my husband tells me I'm beautiful. . .and then he's off searching for his glasses because he can't see the new text on his cell phone.

Let me take you back to elementary school, when girls still played with dolls and boys still had cooties. Around fifth or sixth grade, I stopped eating. From sunup until sunup the following day, I would fast. And it wasn't because I was holy or wanted communion with God.

I would go without food for days at a time because I thought I was fat.

Was I fat? No, not at all. In fact, I was very slim. So where did I get this distorted image?

Maybe it was from television and magazines. Or perhaps from watching my mother practice a continual diet as she exercised with Jack LaLanne. Regrettably for me, I think it went much deeper than that.

I wasn't a Christian as a kid, and therefore I didn't understand that my body was made by God and for God. Moreover, I didn't understand why my body started changing into the beautifully crafted design that God purposed for His glory. A body designed for pleasure (both a husband's pleasure and mine) and for work and for honor and for childbearing.

All I saw were repulsive lumps and bumps and unwanted foreign terrain. My mother noticed my body changing as well. Her advice? "I'd better not catch you kissing any boys!" Actually, really good advice, but did I listen? What do you think? In grammar school I kissed—let's leave it at no matter how many I kissed, I wanted to kiss more.

At the end of elementary school, the popular Mary Beth Smith wrote this in my yearbook: "You're fat, you're ugly, but who the *blip* cares!" Combine encouraging words like that with the memory of tanning at the pool in my bikini as my father's adult male friend gawked at my newly developed body, commenting I had "everything in all the right places," and you now begin to understand my ever-increasing disdain for my almost-grown-up figure.

It took many years to overcome the broken tape playing in my head about body image and self-worth. Every once in a while, the old broken tape plays without my permission, and I have to be deliberate about turning it off. The struggle is real, and I know what it feels like.

A few years back, I strategically tackled all the bad programming, working at it daily, and finally landed on a healthy balance with food and my body. I set out on a mission to eat only when hungry, to consume what I needed for fuel and good health, and to journal daily for a year about how I felt about food, my body, and my overall emotional health. The process was very revealing, and I discovered a lot about myself and having a healthy body image.

But how about you?

Wherever you land on this issue, the most important thing is not to allow inner image struggles to hinder bam-bam in the ham. And with that, let's get to the ham and potatoes, the purpose for which I am writing this book, and hopefully the reason you're reading it: to help you find a sex life in which you are giving yourself completely to your husband—heart, body, mind, and strength. A sex life you love. One that glorifies God despite the negative body images you may have.

You might say, I'd love to be Princess Jasmine (from Disney's *Aladdin*) too, but that just isn't going to happen!

The truth is that it can happen, and it is entirely up to you. You can choose to make it happen. Stay with me as we strip down the issues surrounding this topic and uncover the bare truths at the bottom.

WHAT HE WANTS YOU TO KNOW:

"I love your stomach; it's soft and it's warm. I like a little jiggle—it's womanly."

—Baldwin, married thirty-five years

(If that random quote didn't make sense to you, it's one of the "Anonymous Husbands" quotes you'll see throughout this book; it's stuff husbands would like their wives to know. All names have been changed.)

Remember Who Made You

First, I must remind you: God formed you.

I know you've heard that over and over.

That's all right; here it is again: "You formed my inward parts; You wove me in my mother's womb. I will give thanks to You, for I am fearfully and wonderfully made; wonderful are Your works, and my soul knows it very well" (Psalm 139:13–14).

Don't just read that. Let it sink in. Marinate in it.

God made you just the way you are, for His glory and His use. We all come in different shapes and sizes. In fact, this is something I say to myself when I see someone who looks the way I think *I* should look: "We all come in different shapes and sizes."

Take a look around at all the various shapes and sizes God has made, and remind yourself that God made you and said, "It was very good" (Genesis 1:31).

Be kind to yourself and stop beating yourself up over the parts of your body you don't like.

WHAT HE WANTS YOU TO KNOW:

"I like your extra junk and not just in your trunk. I'm not looking at that. I'm lookin' at the hoo-hoos and bajinga! Extra weight doesn't bother me at all. It's not how big the house is as long as it's painted nice."

—Gabe, middle-aged husband

What's Not to Like?

I've heard women say all kinds of mean things about their bodies.

- "I hate my nose."
- "My hair is too stringy."
- "I know I'm fat."
- "My boobs are awful."
- "My feet are so ugly."
- "I may look good to you, but if you saw me naked you wouldn't say that!"

Even women who to me have seemed confident with their bodies have told me terrible things about their size, shape, or surface. We've all heard the complaints.

Where are we getting this?

Let's go back—way, way back.

Have you seen a picture of the Venus of Willendorf from way before Jesus' time? This sculpture looks like a round sumo wrestler with hazelnuts for boobies; it was an idol symbolizing the ability of a woman's body to swell and bear children. I vote we go back to that! Ancient Greek statues also depicted women with full and luscious bodies.

Curvy was considered attractive in the Renaissance era as well. Moving on to the Elizabethan era, we find full faces, full bodies, and pale skin. Pale skin was a symbol of beauty, class, and wealth, because only poor women had tanned skin, indicating they'd been working outside. (By the 1980s we had tanning salons and women *paid* to look like a "poor working woman." Or we'd slather up our bodies with Coppertone and work to get a tan. I can remember as a teen loading up with baby oil and baking in the sun—in my string bikini—all day, only to show off my dark stomach that night, wearing my white ditto jeans to accent the tan.)

Around 1635 the oil painting *The Three Graces* by Peter Paul Rubens emerged, depicting full-figured women with curves and cellulite. Now that's my jam!

Then *style* took a painful turn for the worse for us women. In the 1890s corsets became wildly popular with the illustrations of the Gibson Girls by Charles Dana Gibson. My guess is that Charles hated women and wanted to torture us. Those corsets were painful and made it hard to breathe, which caused women to faint. Fashion hurts! *Bring back Peter Paul with the cellulite, please.*

In the 1920s the super-slender trend continued with the flappers. The flappers were free and loose with sporty, gender-bending hairstyles, and their dresses featured straight lines. Hey, at least the painful corset was a thing of the past. During the Great Depression from 1929 to 1939, a fuller figure was in. Of course it was—it meant you were actually eating!

And you gotta love Marilyn Monroe rockin' that fuller hour-glass figure from the 1950s to early 1960s. Up next was Lesley Lawson, known as Twiggy, and thin was back in as she strutted her slim stuff on the front of *Vogue* magazine and many others.

The TV show *Charlie's Angels*—welcome, Farrah Fawcett—emerged in the 1970s, and thin was still in, along with not wearing a bra. That was a long hop from the corset era—freedom at last!

In the 1980s, hello, supermodel! Women could easily find many things wrong with their physiques. (What happened to swelling, curves, and a full, luscious figure?) This thin supermodel trend continued through the 1990s with a bump in 1992—move outta the way for Sir Mix-a-Lot's "Baby Got Back (I Like Big Butts)." Piggybacking on Sir Mix-a-Lot, in the 2000s came Kim Kardashian, buttocks first, showcasing her full-size derriere.

Currently (hallelujah!) we are coming to a time when the

media is beginning to celebrate and embrace women of all shapes and sizes. *Peter Paul, I love you and your cellulite paintings!* Unfortunately, we've also perfected our photoshopping techniques so that everyday selfies can look like glamour shots. Cue the sad trumpet, *Wah-wah-waaah.*

Admittedly, we still have a long way to go in this area. Let's face it: the media has been feeding us what we should look like. Ladies, this is madness! We've been fed images of what our bodies are "supposed" to look like, and we are buying into them like a hypnotized sitcom audience.

WHAT HE WANTS YOU TO KNOW:

"Your whole body is a playground to me. If the swing's fat and the slide's curvy, that's okay. I don't care. We men like it all."

—Gus, married with four kids

In *Love and War* by John and Stasi Eldredge, John expresses openly what he wishes his wife knew. He says he desires to see those negligees more often, wants her to initiate more often; even if he's sleeping, he doesn't care—he wants to be woken up. He loves feeling like his wife's hero and wants to know what pleases her, and especially that *he* pleases her.[1]

Looking from a Different Angle

In *Love and War* Stasi Eldredge tells a story about shopping for a honeymoon gift for a friend when she spotted a silky number that reminded her of what she had worn on her own wedding night. As she felt the material of the nightie, she realized it was hanging with the large sizes—1X, 2X, 3X—which was sobering because it was the size she needed. She considered herself majorly overweight and wasn't feeling in control over the battle.

Stasi decided the negligee would look awful on her but tried it on anyway as fast as she could, only looking in the mirror with a quick glance, and hurriedly made the purchase. It had been a very long time since she had bought anything like it.

She waited two weeks before deciding to take the plunge while she and John were away and staying in a hotel room. John was going over notes for the wedding ceremony he'd be officiating the following day, when she went into the bathroom to change. She expresses how nervous she was to put it on, but she had not brought anything else and was completely committed to following through with her initiating on this night. The nightie would send a signal, and she was apprehensive about that. She prayed, asking God for courage and help.

When she emerged from the bathroom, John said, "Oh! Pretty!" and then went back to work. Discouraged and a bit bewildered, she grabbed a magazine and lay on the bed—waiting. After a call came in from their sons (don't the kids always seem to interrupt at just the right time?), she stood by her husband's side of the bed to talk with them. I guess in this case the kids did call at just the right time, because after she hung up the phone, John couldn't take his eyes off her. Things played out as Stasi had hoped, maybe even better. They had a beautiful night.[2]

Despite her body issues, Stasi still allowed herself to venture out of her comfort zone. Are you willing to travel outside of your comfort zone for your husband? Don't fall into the trap of thinking that the way you see yourself is the way your husband sees you. This is a hurdle I've personally had to overcome, and I still need to keep myself in check in this regard.

Be careful not to project your issues onto your husband. If he says you look good, believe him! If you asked your man what he finds attractive about you, his answers might surprise you.

Have You Ever Wondered What Eve Looked Like?

The Bible doesn't give us specifics as to how Eve looked when God *fashioned* her. Knowing His creation so well, God probably excluded this information from His Word on purpose. He knew all of us women would compare ourselves to Eve if she'd been described. Have you ever thought about what Eve looked like naked? Maybe she looked like the Venus of Willendorf. If you are like me, you picture what you consider the ideal woman's physique and then give it straight to Eve. But what if Eve looked like you? You don't know that she didn't. Try giving Eve your body in your mind, and see what happens. (And please don't laugh.)

I'm well aware that as we age we can feel as though things are pointing down that we really don't want to point down. You may feel as though your whole body is going south, but that doesn't mean your attitude has to go there as well. Give yourself a break!

Try this approach for your next "shrimpin' the barbie" occasion: When you are alone with your husband and the clothes start flying, no one is there but the two of you. Just like Adam and Eve. Eve was all Adam had, and you are all your husband has. So let him have it. All of it!

In *Under the Sheets*, Dr. Kevin Leman writes, "I can guarantee, ladies, when your guy has you in the sack, he's not thinking about those little love handles. He's thinking about your breasts, which are now fuller, and another little area that's even more intriguing to him than your thighs, which have their own beauty and enticement for him. If he's thinking about your love handles, then he needs a male engine check because something is wrong with that man."[3]

You could be in the middle of shampooing the wookie when you look down and notice something foreign. Upon further examination, you realize it's a fat roll. You have a fat roll. *Gross!* Don't worry about it. You can't do anything about it now. Push it aside and move on. He's not looking at it. You are! Just move on.

WHAT HE WANTS YOU TO KNOW:

"It's not your body that deters me from wanting you sexually; it's your attitude. I think you are *fine!* It's like Halle Berry forty pounds heavier or the Wicked Witch of the West with a tight body—which one would you rather have?"

—Claude, married twenty-two years

Men seem to universally agree on one critical point: the attitude matters most; it's all about the attitude. Which brings me back to us women and our feelings. Our attitude is greatly dependent on how we are feeling. If we aren't feeling good about ourselves, we tend to take that negativity into our banana-in-the-fruit-salad occasions.

Start looking for what is good about your body and take care of this hot commodity. Be vigilant to take care of yourself and do what makes you feel good. Taking care of you is taking care of your marriage and your sex life. I've wandered into dark places where I stopped taking care of myself. I suffered, my husband suffered, and our relationship suffered. It wasn't fair to him, and it wasn't fair to me.

Please understand, I am not at all saying our relationships are contingent on how we look. But let's face it: when we neglect to care for our bodies, a deeper problem is lurking. Inevitably, it will come out in our attitude, both toward ourselves and toward our husbands.

How you feel about yourself directly impacts how you will respond to your husband. When you value something, you care for it more. Your body is a gift from God, and as such, it needs to be treated with immeasurable worth. You have to make peace with your body and create a safe zone in your bedroom—or wherever. Ahem.

I was shopping and noticed a KY product. It said "Kissable Sensations for the Body." It was on sale. Sales are hard for me to resist.

I bought the KY and placed the product proudly standing at attention on my husband's nightstand next to our bed. Not caring if our kids saw it. (But truthfully, I'm glad they didn't.) I won't provide details here, but let's just say it was more than worth the sale price.

We had fun, yes, until I realized it was sticky. Really sticky. I hate sticky! I decided to try to hide my *severe* discomfort from my husband.

The next day he said to me, "You hated the stickiness, didn't you?"

"Yes! How did you know?"

"Honey, I can tell. I know you tried to hide it, but I knew."

Even though you may think he doesn't feel how uncomfortable you are with your body, or at all during sexy time, he knows. The level at which you are enjoying yourself is quite evident to him. Men are like bloodhounds when it comes to this. All they need is the faintest whiff.

We already talked about how a man desires to please the woman in his life—not just when "playing poker" but in all areas. If you want to seem perfect to him, let him know you are pleased. He will not be completely fulfilled until he feels that you are. If you're not, he will sniff it out. Please don't let "extra" pounds or issues become a barrier between you and your husband. Either lose it or let him use it. Remember, "We men like it all," and "You are *fine!*"

I'm willing to bet your husband would say the same thing about you.

You are *fine!* It is so easy to find the flaws in our figures. Stop looking for the flaws and start looking for what's beautiful and lovely. You may have to start with a cute little freckle on your shoulder or the dimples in your cheeks. Take notice of what is good and continually look for things to add.

Make the decision to believe your husband when he gives you compliments. At the very least, you can head in the direction of acceptance and start searching for what is good about your body instead of squinting through a microscope to find what is "not perfect."

And now. . .

It is time to redefine what the perfect body is. Are you ready?

The perfect body is *your* body. Allow me to repeat that: *the perfect body is your body.*

I can't take credit for this revolutionary idea. I must pass the credit to my sweet husband, who will often tell me that my body is the perfect female body.

Look at it this way: Your body is the only body you will ever have. You might as well decide it is perfect. Make the choice to accept it just as it is, as the body God gave you, and decide it is good. And then offer it to your husband.

Dr. Kevin Leman writes, "The vast majority of men would

rather have a wife who's a little on the plain side but has a sexually available attitude than a drop-dead gorgeous woman who treats her husband like ice, constantly freezing him out."[4]

Let Him Have It

You are all he has. When a little kid with no ice cream sees another kid with ice cream, he doesn't care what flavor it is. He wants some ice cream. Ladies, he doesn't care what flavor it is. He just wants some. You are the only flavor he gets. Please don't freeze him out. Instead, relish him, regardless of your size, shape, or supposed imperfections.

> ## WHAT HE WANTS YOU TO KNOW:
> "Stop beating yourself up in the mirror. I love your body."
>
> —Desmond, understanding and
> still enamored husband

Let the Good Times Roll

Think about riding a roller coaster or letting loose at a rock concert or whatever you were doing the last time you abandoned all reservations. You didn't worry about your body image while you were riding the roller coaster—take this approach with sex.

Imagine how your sex life would change if you loved how you looked and felt completely comfortable with your body. What if you believed your man when he tells you that you are hot and sexy? What if you didn't judge yourself by your physical features but instead looked into his eyes to determine your beauty?

When the bedroom door closes, lock the issues out.

No turning back. Like going down a slide, just let yourself fall.

Fall deeply. Plummet with abandon and pretend you are the only two people on the planet. No barriers, no reluctance. Enjoy him, and celebrate him enjoying you. Accept him. Accept yourself.

Remember, he wants to please you. Do you want a new man? Be a woman he can please and see what happens.

SECRET SEX MISSION #5

This is your mission if you wish to accept it: The next time you're having fun makin' bacon, pay close attention to him. Not to your own body or how you look. Just him. Watch him. Is he enjoying you? Don't allow anything to hinder the intimacy between you and your husband. Make the decision to unconditionally love and accept yourself just the way you are right now.

ASK HIM

Ask your husband for reasons he appreciates your body. What does he like the most? His answers may surprise you.

CHAPTER 6

WHEN ABUSE IS IN YOUR PAST

> NOT TONIGHT, HONEY—
> I NEED TO WASH MY HAIR.

My dad would be defined as a hardworking, determined man. He grew up in project homes in New Jersey, the oldest of four children. After fathering three children, Dad put himself through college, earning a bachelor's degree by taking night classes.

Living in New Jersey meant cold, icy winters, and the definition of a better life to Dad was moving to California. To him, one particular winter seemed colder than the rest.

The year was 1969, and back then, when you bought a car you had to order it and wait for it to come in. While Dad was waiting for his new car to arrive, he decided to make sure he got "the best deal he could" by checking out another dealership. On his way there, he accidentally drove just past it, looked back to gauge his whereabouts, and hit one of the new cars the dealership had parked along the street.

As the salesmen came running out, my dad's words were, "You just lost a sale."

His car was totaled, and he was left without a car for three weeks. In 10-degree weather his route to work started with a fifteen-minute walk to catch a train; then he'd switch to a bus, usually arriving at work about two hours late. At the end of the workday, he did the same and arrived back home late, tired, and cold. He'd joke to us kids about icicles growing off his nose.

Later that year, even though I was only six years old, I

remember Dad barreling through the front door with a bull-horn announcement: "We are moving to California!" He told my mother he was going *no matter what* and she'd best go along with it. There was absolutely no changing his mind.

He sold the family house and bought a 1967 Buick the day the sale of our home closed. The next day my dad, mom, little sister, and I left for California. We made three stops along the way. The first was at the doctor's office because my three-year-old sister had a cold. The second and third stops were to say goodbye to family.

I can still remember the screams and cries of the grandparents, aunts, and uncles we were leaving behind in New Jersey. For me the hardest person to leave behind was my older brother from my dad's first marriage. He would continue to live with his mom in New Jersey. With a packed Buick and my little sister's medication, we drove off, leaving New Jersey behind and heading toward what my dad described as paradise—beautiful, sunny, and "free of bees"—California.

The year 1970 was the year we moved to California. It was also the year I was molested. I was only seven years old.

After a brief stay at a motel, our family rented an apartment in Canoga Park. It wasn't exactly what my parents were used to in our quaint little house in Iselin, New Jersey, but we were in the fairy-tale world of sun and famous people and a new life without snow or icy streets.

I do not have a clear memory of what happened to me while we lived in that apartment building—it wasn't until I was in my forties that I even realized I had been molested. One day while I was working with children at my church, I looked at a little seven-year-old girl and thought to myself, *The memories I have are not normal.* More specifically, the "memories" were secrets. Secrets that I had told no one—not even my husband.

The shame and regret I carried were way too heavy to share. I couldn't bear the idea of releasing those "secrets." As a result, I bottled them up, trying desperately to forget them.

While my family lived in that apartment "paradise," I made friends with an "older" girl who was eight years old. Her name was Tami. She was my best friend at the time, and we shared many things. Primarily, we shared the same secret.

There was this "game" Tami and I liked to play. Running, we would go up the stairs, turn right, run straight ahead, and knock on the door in the corner. Once inside, I can remember being in a bedroom. What happened in that bedroom never should have happened. My memory is not exactly clear, but I remember enough to know it was not something a seven-year-old should have experienced. This was a "game" we played willingly, and we visited this apartment on a regular basis.

Since I had gone there willingly, looking at it as a game, I felt it was my fault. I carried that feeling into adulthood, along with other incidents that had accumulated over the years, burying all the shame and guilt and regret in a chest of secrets.

I met my husband when I was seventeen years old, and we married two weeks after my nineteenth birthday. In my early twenties, I became a Christian. It wasn't until I had been married for more than twenty-five years that I began considering telling my husband about my humiliating and deeply hidden secrets.

One day while my husband and I were sitting on our front porch enjoying the evening breeze, gathering all the courage I could grasp, I blurted, "I think I was molested." There. It was out. For the first time ever. He hardly reacted. He simply said, "Hmm, okay."

Feeling safe, I continued and relayed my story—my secret—and he listened tenderly. When I was finished, I said, "So, I think I was molested." He said, "Yes, it sounds to me like you definitely were."

That was pretty much it. He didn't love me any less. He didn't judge me. He didn't think any less of me. For him it was just another day not much different than any other day. As usual, he displayed kindness, love, and understanding, but for me it was a monumental day. It was the day my secret no longer haunted me. It had been released, holding me captive no more—I was finally free.

I began sharing my story with trusted friends. Sadly, and surprisingly, several of them had their own to tell.

One friend whom I dearly love shared her story with me. She is one of the most genuine, kind, and loving people you could ever hope to meet. She wrote out her story for me and has allowed me to share it with you. (Names have been changed.)

Jessica's Story

My misconceptions about sex started in childhood. When I was six years old, my brother Todd, who was nearly ten years older than I was, called me into his room one evening after I had taken my bath. I was in my pajamas ready for bed. He began coaxing me to pull down my underwear because he wanted to "see our differences." With much resistance, I finally gave in. It was a short "show and tell" interaction.

About a year later, my parents separated, and one of my mother's friends was babysitting me. She had a daughter who was two years older than I was, and while we were playing house (I was the baby), she decided it was time for feeding. She raised her shirt and stuck her tiny breast in my mouth and told me to suck on it like a little baby would. I was totally freaked out.

When my mom came to pick me up, I was crying and I told her I didn't want to stay there anymore. I never told her why, but luckily we never went back.

The next incident occurred after we moved in with my mom's

new boyfriend, Ben. I was alone flipping channels on the television and stopped on a channel where two people were having sex. After a few minutes, my mom came running in and turned it off. She told me I wasn't supposed to watch that and sent me outside.

We eventually moved into our own house, but Ben stayed over often. Todd, my older brother, would babysit me during the day. I have very bad memories of my brother, mostly of him being mean and yelling at my mother and me.

The worst memory of Todd was a time he was in his bed naked and said he wanted to play house, and that I could be the mommy. He lured me into his bed and took off my clothes. I was only eight years old. He was kissing me and touching me everywhere and wanting me to touch him. He got on top of me and pressed up and down. My legs were closed and there was no penetration. He did coax me into performing oral sex on him, though. That is the hardest thing for me to get over; it is hard to understand why I would do that. I think I wanted his affection even though he always treated me like he hated me.

Shortly after this, my nightmares began. I would wake up crying but was too scared to go to my mom. The only way to my mom's room was through my brother's room, and that was way too risky.

However, one nightmare was too intense, and I decided to stealthily creep to my mom's room. After I had successfully passed through my brother's room and peeked through the crack of the door of Mom's room, I realized Ben was staying over. I could see my mother reading a magazine, but Ben was lying on his back touching his penis and quickly moving his hand up and down. I was extremely scared and ran back to my room.

From that point on, I dealt with the nightmares on my own, usually by clenching stuffed animals and hiding under covers tightly tucked around me. A few years later, I learned to defeat the nightmares through prayer.

At twelve years old, I began experimenting, playing "show and tell" with friends, while our parents socialized in the other room.

When I was thirteen years old, my mother decided to sit me down and try to have "the talk" with me. I cried. She ended up handing me some books and told me I could go to her if I had any questions. She asked me if anyone had ever touched me inappropriately. I lied.

By the age of fifteen, I had become a professional liar, automatically telling people what I thought they wanted to hear.

I didn't tell anyone my secret, but as a teenager I did make a feeble attempt to tell some friends one night while we were driving around. The subject of sex came up, and I tested the waters. I told them I had French kissed a boy. When they asked, "Who?" I jokingly said, "My brother." The response was a repulsed "Ewwww" by all. From that moment on, I vowed to keep my dirty little secret until death.

That same year, my mom decided it was time for me to be on birth control. Being protected from pregnancy, I was even more determined to have sex. That way I could have true stories to tell my friends instead of the lies I had been telling them.

I finally had intercourse at the age of eighteen with a boy I had been dating for only two months. We both had grown up in the church. Basically, I was shocked by how sex worked. He noticed my confusion and asked what was wrong. I simply stated I didn't know it actually worked like that (meaning the actual penetration). He just gave me a weird look and resumed. It was Mother's Day.

I had led him to believe he was my first, although I didn't feel it was true. My virginity had been stolen from me at an early age.

I never felt it was a special gift I could give my husband on our wedding night.

Finally, I did not have to lie about sex anymore. I felt liberated and free. I would no longer feel rejected when I tried to tell the truth about my sexual history, or worse, relive the experiences of the past through lies.

I found some comfort in telling my boyfriend about being abused by my brother. He sympathized with me and shared in my pain.

While at church, we both went forward during an altar call. I can remember being surrounded by people from the church while we cried. We both knew our relationship was not what God intended. After we broke up, I discovered he had cheated on me. I felt so betrayed; we had been together for two years.

Shortly after being baptized, I told my parents what my brother had done to me as a kid. They both were very understanding. I was "good" for about a month. Then I began to live two lives. One life was the good newly baptized girl. The other was a life filled with drinking, partying, and sex.

Then one night I hit an all-time low. I was lying in bed with my boyfriend at the time, in a ratty trailer in the middle of nowhere. We had been partying. I could see the moon out of the small window above the bed as flies buzzed around the room. A fly crawled across my lip, and that was it. I jumped up and shouted, "I want out!" I ended the relationship the next day.

Not long after, I started dating Victor, who today is my husband of more than twenty-five years. When Victor and I got together, we had an instant connection, talking for hours at a time. About a month into our relationship, we started having sex. I had adopted a "why not" attitude toward sex. I felt I had blown the whole virginity thing, and having sex was just like grabbing a bite to eat together. Less than a year later, we were married.

In the beginning, our sex life was somewhat new and exciting. Sex without guilt was a bit more enjoyable. A few times we spent all weekend in bed with short breaks for food and sleep. It was fun, and we had been given license to do it as much as we wanted without being rebuked by family, friends, or church people.

The irony was that even with those weekends filled with sex, in reality I was having a difficult time adjusting to life as a wife. The rest of the time, I was coming out of the shower fully dressed, mortified at the thought of him seeing me completely naked. I was always careful to adjust the covers on our bed so that I was never completely uncovered.

He would bombard me with questions about sex, what I liked or didn't like. My thinking was, *We just had sex! Can't you just be happy with that?* I didn't realize his intent was to help our sex life grow into something that I actually enjoyed. For me, sex was a chore. I think he began to feel like a Viking, ravaging and pilfering a small village. Or maybe that's how I felt and projected it onto him.

We began to be more active at church, and I developed a desire to live a godly life. What I heard from the "godly" women at church was that sex was a chore. Their men wanted it all the time, much to their chagrin. In their eyes, men were pigs. The women maintained that the missionary position was the only godly way to have sex, and that it was only for procreation. I was becoming more and more confused, and Victor continued to try to get me to talk about our sex life, or lack thereof.

Finally, I confided in Victor about being sexually abused by my brother. He consoled me and told me I never had to do anything I was uncomfortable doing. He put my needs before his and was very understanding and compassionate—letting me know we didn't have to have sex unless I wanted to.

Unfortunately, I used this as a way to get out of sex. He

became increasingly sexually frustrated, which led to frequent arguments about unrelated topics. I felt he was being a barbarian. He felt I was being a prude.

Victor continued to try to talk to me about sex. Being too embarrassed and ashamed, instead of talking I would sit motionless with tears trickling down my cheeks, feeling filled with fear and shame.

Desperate, Victor went to his *grandmother* for sex advice. Grandma was the godliest woman I've ever known, and her advice was, "All things done in private between a husband and wife is glory to God." My rebuttal was, "Even if he wants me to swing from the chandelier?!" She laughed and said, "Yes, even swinging from the chandelier."

Later Victor and I had a more heartfelt discussion about sex. He held me and told me he loved my body. I was quick to state that he had never really seen all of me. He said, "Jess, we've been married for a while now—I've seen your body." I laughed, somewhat embarrassed, realizing that all my covert ops to hide myself from him had been in vain.

I felt safe when he held me, knowing all my secrets and loving me in spite of them. Since then, I have started kicking out all the people who have haunted our bedroom in my mind, including my brother and all others who gave me an ungodly and twisted view of sex.

For years I prayed for God to bless our marriage and our friendship. Now I include our sex life too, having a clearer perspective of what God intends for us.

I've also realized that the more I bust down the walls and misconceptions about sex, the greater our love for each other grows. I have become more vocal about my likes and dislikes in the bedroom, and it has improved our sex life dramatically. This has deepened our relationship and our conversations.

Once you've discussed the most private part of your relationship, discussing other things is easy. I've also noticed that my husband is happier when he knows he is pleasing me in the bedroom, and I'm happier when I allow myself to get lost in him.

About two weeks after receiving Jessica's story, I received an email from her:

> Lu, after sharing my story with you, it continued to resonate with me. I couldn't let it go. Emotions and anger were building up in me. I picked a fight with my husband. I told him he never made me feel like I was ever going to be enough. Then I turned my frustration and anger toward God. I felt my spirit cry out to Him, "What more do You want from me?!"
>
> My reply came quickly. God told me, "I want ALL of you."
>
> That night I couldn't sleep and cried out to God once more. He showed me that I needed to really face the truth of what had happened to me and really come to terms with what that eight-year-old child had endured.
>
> Since I have let out my story, both with you and my husband, and was truly honest with myself, facing what actually happened, I've discovered a newfound freedom. I have a peace I have never known before. I never realized until now that I had been carrying a lot of shame and hatred toward myself. I actually feel like a weight has been lifted.

Another change that has occurred is a physical change in my body. For the first time in my life, I had a full menstrual cycle without the help of birth control. My cycle began the day after I allowed myself to face the truth about my past.

I'm still working through all of this, but I can't deny the fact that I definitely feel more at peace with myself and much more joyful lately. If you take anything from my story, I hope it is this: never stop asking the tough questions. Asking me the tough key questions about my story was the springboard that pushed me to face the truth. I am all the better for it.

Do You Have a Story?

How about you? Do you have your own story? Maybe you're like I was and don't think you have a story. I didn't think so. The more I learned about what is defined as sexual abuse according to the experts, the more I found incidents from my childhood that would qualify. Not unlike Jessica, I had to allow God to reveal the past encounters I had locked tightly inside and face the truth about each situation.

To move forward on the path to healing, acknowledge each assault against you. Recognize it for what it is and give it to God. Allow God to heal you. Embrace that helpless, powerless little girl. Protect, defend, and comfort her.

Jesus said, "For nothing is hidden, except to be revealed; nor has anything been secret, but that it would come to light" (Mark 4:22). Until we are honest with ourselves and with God—who already knows everything—we will never fully break free from our destructive patterns. Victims develop coping mechanisms in childhood to deal with the painful, confusing, and shameful things that happened. They switch to autopilot, acting out in unhealthy ways and not understanding why.

Maybe you have an aversion to sex. Have you ever thought about that?

Maybe you battle with bulimia, which is not uncommon for individuals who suffered sexual abuse as children. That was one of my coping mechanisms. Fortunately, I was able to find good professional help in my early twenties, stop the destructive pattern, and find freedom, but I never knew the root of it until I better understood the effects of sexual abuse.

Maybe you drink too much, work too much, eat too much. Maybe you are a sex addict. Maybe you tease men—entering into relationships only to hurt them. Maybe you're a control freak—if it's not your way, then someone has to pay. Maybe. . . maybe. . .you fill in the blank.

Dr. Dan B. Allender writes in his book on childhood sexual abuse, *The Wounded Heart*, "The sexually abused person is in a war. The enemy is ultimately the Evil One and the path of loyalty to Satan's vision: rebellion, autonomy, or in other words, sin. The dilemma is that Satan is crafty and his path is often subtle."[1]

Coping with the effects of sexual abuse can be like fighting an invisible enemy, swinging madly and falling down, trying to mend your brokenness without a clear focus on what or who the enemy is or what it is you are fighting for or against. In the end, you are left feeling defeated, shattered, and hopeless.

At the very least, when you recognize and face what happened to you, then you can begin to deal with it.

Facing the Truth about Your Past

Sometimes facing the truth means acknowledging that an adult whom we love either hurt us or didn't protect us from hurt. For many, this reality can be too painful to face. As a child, trying to put together *Mommy and Daddy love me and take care of me* and *Mommy and Daddy hurt me or didn't protect me from being hurt* is too great a task. Consequently, the child concludes, *There must be something wrong with me. I am at fault, and I must keep this a secret.* Sadly, we take this unfortunate mind-set into adulthood.

Secrets are never good. Secrets enable an abuser to continue in destructive patterns. Victims of sexual abuse keep secrets for a multitude of reasons. Many children view secrecy as their only choice to avoid punishment. And many adults maintain secrets to keep from feeling even more shame than they already carry. In the book *No Place to Cry*, Doris Van Stone writes about the pain she experienced when her husband passed away, having felt he was the only person who truly loved her. Having been physically and sexually abused as a child, she describes feeling dirty, ashamed, and unworthy of love from another. She explains that no matter how much she tried to seem normal to others, she felt different inside, and felt as if everyone knew it.[2]

How do you break free from the secrets of your past?

Your first step is to devote yourself to truth. A secret holds you captive. It provides shame a place of residence inside your heart and soul. Consequently, you need to open the door of your heart, kick out every secret, and slam the door shut. Tell someone you trust. Tell your husband, or tell a counselor. Don't hold it in anymore where it continues to wreak havoc in your heart and in your life.

Now, I'm not suggesting you raise your hand in the middle of church and proclaim you have an announcement to make. Yes, tell others, but carefully select *whom* you will tell and *when*. Choose only those you can trust.

Facing the truth is the first step on the path toward wholeness. Face the truth about your past. Be honest about what really happened to you as a child. Don't hold on to a sugarcoated version.

A Night of Healing

I carefully selected six women to invite to my home for a night of food, sharing, and complete acceptance. Each of these dear ladies had confided in me about their past sexual abuse as children. I told each to bring pictures of themselves during the time the abuse was happening and let them know we'd all be sharing our stories.

I made a traditional Italian dinner, and after eating to our hearts' content, we took turns sharing what had happened to us as children. We each created our own timeline with pictures symbolizing the years our abuse took place. The pictures were filled with innocent little girls, and the room was filled with comforting tears. One by one each woman told her story. One by one each woman received understanding, sympathy, and empathy. It was a night of great healing. We not only accepted each other; we accepted ourselves. Interestingly, the six of us came to an odd universal realization. We all thought our own abuse wasn't as bad as that of the others. We'd all minimized what had happened to us, thinking the others had suffered more than we had.

In many cases, adult victims minimize their past abuse, viewing it through the eyes of an adult. "It really wasn't that bad," they'll say. Or even worse, they convince themselves it was their fault because they were "willing" victims, or they didn't fight hard enough, or somehow they lured their perpetrator, or, or, or, or. . .

Insert whatever you want, but there is *never* a reason an innocent child is to blame for endured abuse. You are not to blame. It's not your fault.

Turning from Unhealthy Protection Patterns

As I mentioned earlier, as children we develop coping mechanisms to deal with what happened to us. While this is a natural response for a child, those mechanisms may develop into unhealthy patterns that will later need to be broken. Look for unhealthy protection patterns or coping mechanisms you may have carried into adulthood. Open your eyes to destructive behaviors by which you may be hurting yourself or others.

In *The Wounded Heart*, Dr. Dan Allender says, "Often the abuse victim realizes that the same patterns that allowed the abuse to occur and go unaddressed are equally operative in her life today. Victimization is usually not only an event in the past; in most cases, it is an ongoing, day-by-day experience."[3]

Don't allow your past to dictate your future. Put an end to any destructive behavior. It could manifest itself as an eating disorder, a dysfunctional relationship, alcoholism, a phobia, sexual unresponsiveness, promiscuity, uncontrollable rage, a critical demeanor—the list goes on and on.

In their book *Breaking Free*, Carolyn Ainscough and Kay Toon explain that sometimes victims feel compelled to act out in various ways, such as masturbating over and over, or continuing to engage in sexual acts in an effort to deter thoughts and feelings about past abuse. Some may only be able to obtain pleasure from certain practices like using objects, or being tied up, or wanting pain to be inflicted, or even *causing* physical pain to another. Many times these sexual preferences are reflective of what has happened to them during times of abuse—one's own sexual abuse history is acted out through their current sexual behavior.[4]

In an attempt to avoid more emotional pain, victims typically create unhealthy self-protective patterns, treating themselves and sometimes others in unloving, destructive ways.

Steven Tracy writes in his book *Mending the Soul* that sexual abuse sometimes creates shame in the victims to the point where they interpret normal sexual urges and marital sex as shameful. Physical pleasure can feel "unsafe" or "dirty." Body loathing also may occur, or victims may behave destructively through self-starvation or self-injury. Instead of rejecting physical pleasure, as many sadly do, Tracy implores abuse victims to embrace love and sexuality as beautiful expressions of God's design.[5]

Overcoming this kind of loathing toward sex and sexuality can prove difficult and may require professional help. I encourage you to do whatever you need to do to begin the healing process.

Opening Your Heart to Trust and Love Others

Trusting another person can be extremely challenging, especially when trusting or being coerced by someone in the past is what caused so much pain. Nonetheless, a big step in healing is learning to trust and love other people. This step may feel dangerous. You may need to be guarded as you open your heart to love and trust, knowing that you could be hurt once again. We're never guaranteed that everything will work out perfectly. However, the huge difference is that you now have an adult to look out for you, and that adult is you.

Protect yourself like you would your own daughter. Station an imaginary armed guard around the perimeter of your life, letting good things in and halting anything unwanted or harmful. Exercise using the word *no*, and surround yourself with people who gracefully receive the word *no*. In their book *Boundaries*, Dr. Henry Cloud and Dr. John Townsend write that we can't change people, but we can limit our exposure to those who behave poorly.[6]

Protect yourself, but do not isolate yourself. Part of protecting yourself is connecting with people you can trust, people who are safe. Don't be afraid to love people. Allowing yourself to be loved and fervently loving others will enable you to make big strides along the healing path. Get in the game of love.

Loving people is something God clearly instructs us to do:

"And He [Jesus] said to him, "'You shall love the LORD your God with all your heart, and with all your soul, and with all your mind.' This is the great and foremost commandment. The second is like it, 'You shall love your neighbor as yourself'" (Matthew 22:37–39). Don't guard your heart so closely that you miss out on the blessing of loving others and allowing others to love you. God made us with the desire for connectedness, a gift we need to embrace fully.

Forgiving Yourself and Others

Forgive yourself. Even though abuse victims are just that—victims—which by definition means "not at fault," oftentimes they carry baseless blame.

Forgive. Release your perception of being too weak, too foolish, too scared, or too permissive. Forgive yourself for the unjust perception that your normal, God-given desires for intimacy and love were like a web that lured you in and entrapped you. Forgive yourself for any acting out you may have done, and for any unhealthy self-protection patterns.

Sometimes victims have a hard time forgiving themselves because they may have enjoyed certain aspects of the abuse. Please understand: God created us to love human touch and attention. It feels good. Receiving "extra" attention can make us feel special. God made us as sexual beings, beings who enjoy physical touch and closeness. It is excruciatingly difficult to accept that we received any pleasure from such perverse acts. In the end, we are forced to conclude there must be something wrong with us and everything that happened was our fault. But this conclusion is blatantly untrue.

You were a victim.

Forgive all persons responsible for the mistreatment you undeservedly endured. Forgive the people who were supposed to protect you. Personally, I know this step can be very difficult. Yet when we release all of our hurt and anger to God, and forgive the people involved in our abuse, we are then set free.

It helps if you are able to view the abuser as a human for whom Christ died—a sinner just like you who needs God's forgiveness, mercy, and grace. The Bible gives us a great example of God's mercy in the story of Jonah and the people of Nineveh (see Jonah 3-4). God makes His salvation available to all. No one is beyond the grasp of God's supernatural love and forgiveness.

No one can make you forgive. That is entirely up to you. However, if you choose to feed any animosity lurking in your heart, the only person who will be hurt is you. You are only jailing yourself, becoming your own cruel prison guard. Let yourself out of prison and forgive. It starts with a decision; your feelings will follow. Eventually.

Keep in mind that forgiving does not mean we continue to allow an abuser to hurt or mistreat us. Forgiveness is a kindness we give ourselves by letting go of any resentment.

As we put our past to rest—by dealing with it and facing the truth—we can then move on to the future God has for us.

Moving On

It's time to gather the manna. God provided manna for His people (see Exodus 16). Each day the Israelites had to gather enough manna for that day. God dropped it from the sky, but *they had to gather it*! He didn't force them to eat it. They could have rejected it and left it there. It was their choice to gather what they needed. Likewise, it is our choice to gather what God provides for us.

The manna is a picture of what God does for us each day. Jehovah Jireh (God our Provider) sends us unconditional love, acceptance, grace, and mercy every day. We need to gather it every day like the Israelites did the manna. There is enough for each day, but we need to pick it up.

We can cry out to God, handing Him our hurts, needs, innermost desires, insecurities—all of our overwhelming feelings. Ask God to heal you and give you all you need and long for. And then wait and trust. He will answer.

Your answer may be the ability to get through another day. Your answer may come through a loving Christian brother or sister, or through a verse that pops out at you. It may be a clear direction from God to take action or to reach out for help from others. It could be as simple as a feeling of peace, the kind of peace only God can give.

God is always waiting for us and interested in our hurts and needs. "Be anxious for nothing, but in everything by prayer and supplication with thanksgiving let your requests be made known to God. And the peace of God, which surpasses all comprehension, will guard your hearts and your minds in Christ Jesus" (Philippians 4:6–7).

Sexual abuse perverts what God meant for beauty. It distorts what God meant for good and for love. Let God rescue you from your past, and give Him your future. He'll take what's broken, put it back together, and create something beautiful—something that brings Him glory. Give all of your brokenness to God.

Do you believe God can restore you? He can. Will you trust Him? It is our job to pick up our manna. Rely on the sufficiency of Jehovah Jireh.

I sincerely hope the subject matter of this chapter does not apply to you; however, if it did, and it brought up painful memories, I am truly sorry. Please know that I hurt deeply with you. And please understand that molestation implants the lie that sex is something you shouldn't enjoy. Satan seeks to steal and destroy and wants to rob you of the precious gift of oneness that God provides. Please accept God's gift.

SECRET SEX MISSION #6

This is your mission if you wish to accept it: Is anything holding you back from fully enjoying your physical relationship with your husband? Take the necessary steps to enhance your love life. Like Jessica (her story is at the beginning of this chapter), kick out all of the people who haunt your bedroom. If you have flashbacks, remind yourself that you are an adult and that oneness is a precious gift from God. Seek help if you need it—join a survivors group or reach out to a therapist.

ASK HIM

Openly communicate to your husband any past experiences that are holding you back from fully embracing your sexual relationship.

PART 3

UNDERSTANDING HIS SEXUALITY

CHAPTER 7

A DAY IN THE LIFE OF A HUSBAND

> NOT TONIGHT, HONEY—
> I NEED TO UPDATE MY FACEBOOK.

Say hello to Mr. John Johnson. He's a regular guy, with a pretty wife, three kids, a beagle, a mortgage, and two car payments. Our story begins with the glorious sound of the alarm clock at 6:00 a.m. As John turns off his alarm, he peers over at his wife. He thinks to himself, *She is so beautiful even as she sleeps.* He lifts up the covers to a sea of cotton. Her favorite full-length rose-tinted cotton gown flows from her top to her bottom. *Not my favorite, but I do love the body under all that granny gown.* He's been wanting to tell her how much he hates it but doesn't want to hurt her feelings. He knows it's her favorite. Cozy. Warm. Comfortable. She tells him often.

As John looks at her, his desire for her grows. Starting at her feet, he slowly caresses her leg. She rolls away from him. "I was up late last night," she mumbles. "I'm tired."

Discouraged, John gets out of bed. *Maybe tonight.*

While in the shower, he thinks about ripping the nightgown to shreds and carrying his wife into the shower with him. . .like Tarzan. Yeah, like Tarzan. Suddenly his wife's razor falls to the shower floor and he grabs the ledge, trying not to fall, but his foot slips and his body bangs against the tile. Ouch!

As he towels off, he can see a bruise forming on his hip. *What happened to that free-spirited, adventurous young guy? I climbed Mount Whitney. I used to play basketball half the night with my buddies. I could bow-chick-a-wow-wow half the night. What hap-pened to that guy?*

John quietly finishes getting ready, and before heading out he sees his wife is waking up and gives her a kiss goodbye. He heads out, and she heads to get the kids up.

As John opens the door to his routine coffee stop, he sees an attractive woman walking in behind him. *Wow, she is stunning!* He elects to hold the door open for her, like a gentleman. As she passes, he is careful to keep his eyes fixed beyond her firm frame. "Thank you," she says with a soft voice. John nods. Stand-ing in line behind her, he notices her sheer blouse tucked neatly into her skirt. *I can't wait to get home to my wife.*

John approaches the counter to order his espresso, and his cell phone rings. As he looks down at his phone and glances back at the barista, he notices her bright purple bra peeking out from the top of her blouse. He looks back at his phone and sees it's Stan who's calling. He answers it.

"Stan, did you find out? Wait, wait."

Looking back at the pretty barista, he mumbles, "I apologize for the phone." Clearing his throat and keeping his eyes from looking down, he says, "Can I get a double double? I mean a dou-ble espresso, please?"

He returns to his phone. "Stan, what did you find out?"

"John, it's true! There are going to be top-level layoffs today. I think it's—"

"Sir, excuse me," the barista says. "You need to pay."

"What?"

"Sir, you need to pay for your espresso."

"Stan, hold on."

As he fumbles around to grab his card, John's cell slips out of his hand and crashes to the floor.

"That ain't good," says the spunky barista.

John picks up his cell. "Stan? Stan? Dang!"

John grabs his coffee and rushes out. *What if my job is on the line? I can't lose my job.*

Walking to his car, he can feel his heart racing to a dangerous level. *I can't wait for this day to be over. I can't wait to get home to my wife.*

He finally arrives at work, parks quickly, and hurriedly walks to the elevator. He pushes the button, and in seconds the elevator door opens. As he enters the elevator, he sees a woman bent over fixing her shoe. As she stands, he sees it's Vanessa, Christine's assistant. "Good morning, Mr. Johnson. Christine is looking for you. She says it's urgent."

Vanessa is gorgeous and sweet. It's too bad her husband is such an idiot. Some guys just don't realize what a great thing they have.

"John, isn't this your floor?"

"Oh, so it is! Thank you."

Vanessa smiles as he walks off the elevator.

I can't wait to get home to my wife.

As he turns the corner, he hears whispers coming from the group of female employees gathered around Caroline, the company receptionist.

"Good morning, ladies."

All in unison: "Good morning, Mr. Johnson."

Caroline says, "Christine needs to talk to you right away, Mr. Johnson."

As he walks away, he can hear whispers again. As he passes Christine's office on the way to his own, she sees him and jumps out of her chair. He can't help but notice that her skirt has a slit running up the side of her leg.

"Good morning, John. I need to talk with you."

Christine follows John into his office and closes the door behind her.

"John, I found out from Vanessa that you are being let go today."

"What?"

"Yes, you know your 3:00 with Mr. Winlock? Well. . ."

"How do you know this?"

"Vanessa."

"How does Vanessa know?"

"She found out from Mary."

"How does Mary know?"

"The bookstore."

"What?"

"She found out from Pete and Rob."

"What? They *told* her?"

"No. She read their lips."

"She read their lips?"

"I know it's true. She's really good at reading lips; she was deaf for years."

"I get it." He paused. "I need some time to think. Thank you, Christine. I really appreciate you telling me."

"Of course, you know I have your back. You stepped up for me when that rumor about me surfaced. It's the least I can do."

"Thank you."

"Sure. I'll let you know if I hear anything else." As Christine leaves to return to her office, Charlotte walks in looking as sharp as always.

John greets her. "Good morning, Charlotte."

"Good morning, boss. I updated your calendar for today. Would you like me to hold your calls?"

"Yes, please." John has always been able to count on Charlotte. She is the best assistant he's ever had.

"How's your mother doing?" John asks.

"Oh, so much better. Thank you for letting me leave early

yesterday to go see her."

"Well, I'm glad she's doing better."

"The doctor said her discomfort was part of normal recovery after such a major surgery. So that was a relief."

"Good. Can you close my door on the way out and mark me as busy until three o'clock, please?"

Charlotte walks toward the door. "No problem." She turns and smiles. "Let me know if you need anything." She closes the door. John listens to the sound of her heels as she walks away.

What am I going to do? Should I call my wife? No. Don't want to worry her. I can deal with this. I can deal with this. I need to figure something out before three o'clock.

John can hear the sound of his heartbeat. He takes deep breaths to calm down. *I can't wait to get home to my wife.*

John sits at his desk and cringes at the pile of messages stacked neatly next to his phone. *Don't need to return those calls. It's gonna be a long day.*

Instead of digging into his work like he usually does, John sits paralyzed, zombie-like, unsure of what to do.

An hour passes.

Two hours.

Suddenly there's a knock on the door.

"Yes?"

Christine enters with Mary, Vanessa, Stan, and Stephanie close behind.

As they take a seat, Stephanie breaks the silence. "I did some digging. Mr. Winlock was given an ultimatum by the Dragon Lady. If numbers didn't rise by the third quarter, he had to let go of somebody. Maybe if you ask for another quarter to get numbers up, he'll reconsider."

John casually sits back in his chair. His knee shakes.

He takes a deep breath. "I know Winlock. He'd never risk taking a chance."

Mary chimes in. "They really need help over at the Lincoln Park building. You could switch departments."

"I might be able to move things around in my department," Stan says.

"Thank you. I appreciate your concern, but I'll be fine."

"Either way," Stan says, trying to relieve some of the tension, "let's all meet up at McGee's tonight after work. You in, John?"

"Yeah," John says. "Probably. Why not? Sure."

Downtrodden, the ladies and Stan head out, except Christine lags behind. "You're such a team player, and all the staff love you. We're going to miss you."

"Thank you, Christine," John says as Christine uncrosses her legs to get up to leave.

What am I going to do? I just want this day to be over so I can go home to my wife.

John spends the rest of his day going through emails and files. With 3:00 p.m. slowly creeping near, John feels his body stiffening.

And then, finally, it's time. He heads to the elevator and goes up a floor.

With his heart racing and his body feeling old, he makes his way down the long hallway.

"Mr. Winlock is waiting for you." Stephanie tries to smile but can't.

As John walks through the door, he feels his heartbeat accelerating even more. *Breathe.*

"John, I've been reviewing your files. . ."

Here it comes. John hears his heart beating dangerously loud.

"I'm promoting you to VP of operations."

Silence.

How is this possible? What did he just say? Act cool and collected.

"Oh. Thank you."

"I'll brief you tomorrow. My kid's got another baseball game."

As John walks down the hall headed back to his office, he stands a bit taller and broader.

I can't wait to get home and tell my wife.

Christine, Stan, Mary, and Vanessa follow John back into his office. John is smiling.

"What happened?" Christine demands.

"I got promoted to VP."

"Yes!" Christine shouts. "So much for rumors."

Mary inquires, "What about the Dragon Lady? Does she know?"

"Mary, please," Vanessa chimes in. "Nothing happens without her consent around here."

Christine confirms, "She was very happy with that last project you did, John, and I'm sure she's heard how the staff love working with you. I know I told her."

John pauses. "Wow, thank you!"

"We definitely need to go celebrate tonight after work," Christine says, hoping John will join them this time. "You in?"

John says, "How could I not?"

As they all leave, John sits back in his chair and spins around like a five-year-old child.

That Christine is so thoughtful. I love working here.

John digs into his work with renewed vigor. He decides to wait and tell his wife the good news in person. *I can't wait to get home to my wife.*

At 5:04 p.m., there's a knock on John's door.

"Yes?"

The door flies open. Christine, Mary, Vanessa, and Stan come racing through.

Stan enters dancing and singing, "Cel-e-brate good times, come on!"

John laughs.

"Ready to go?" Vanessa asks.

"First"—John clears his throat—"I want to say thank you to all of you for your support."

Christine jumps in, covering the awkward silence. "Sure thing! Anything for you—you know we're a team."

"Well, thank you all. But I'll meet you there. I've really got to get this finished. Now go on, I'll catch up."

Stan leaves dancing.

Finally, it's 6:00 p.m. *I am heading home to my wife. I can't wait any longer. Oh wait, I said I'd meet up with them. I'll text Stan. They'll understand.*

Driving home, John's mind wanders as he mulls over the events of the day. His attention is drawn to a woman jogging on the side of the road. *I can't wait to get home to my wife.*

He dials home. No answer.

Then his phone rings. With excitement, he pushes the button to answer and hear his wife on the other end, but instead he hears a different familiar voice reverberating through his car speakers. "Johnny? Are you there?"

It's his mother. *How does she always know when I'm in my car on my way home?*

"Hi, Mom."

"Hello, Johnny, it's Mom."

"Yes, I know—I just said, 'Hi, Mom.' How are you, Ma?"

"Johnny, I'm fine. But your father? Did I tell you we took him back to the doctor? He was getting dizzy, and the doctor told him to cut his heart pills in half." She'd told him the story twice already, but he didn't have the heart to tell her.

"Dizzy, huh?"

"Yeah. Johnny, have you had your cholesterol checked lately? You'd better have it checked. Uncle Jack's got that calonary thing."

"A what?" John asked.

"What?" his mom asked.

"I think I'm fine, Mom."

"When was the last time you were checked?"

"Pretty sure it was last year."

"Well, you'd better go back and get it checked again. What were your numbers when you went?"

"Ma, I'm driving. I don't remember my numbers."

"What? You don't know your numbers? The doctor says that everyone should know their numbers. It's very important, you know. High cholesterol runs in our family, Johnny."

"Okay, Ma."

"Call tomorrow and make an appointment. And get your prostate checked while you're there too. Lots of men have problems with their prostate, you know. Sally's husband is having problems with his prostate."

"Ma, can we talk about this later?"

"Why? What's wrong? Is something wrong? Did something happen?"

"No. I really can't wait to hear about Sally's husband's prostate, but it's been a really long day, and I have to get up early tomorrow to—"

"What? What's happening tomorrow? Is something happening? What's wrong?"

"Mom! Nothing is wrong. I'm just tired. Actually, I got a promotion today, and I'm headed home to tell Sandra about it. So don't call and tell her."

"Why would I do that?"

"I don't know. Why would you tell your granddaughter that you and Dad were dying because we don't visit enough?"

"Does this promotion mean more stress? Because stress kills, you know."

"It's all good, Mom. Nothing to worry about."

"Are you still coming over this weekend?"

"Sure."

"I guess we can celebrate then. Bye, sweetheart. I love you."

"Bye, Ma. Love you too."

"And get your cholesterol checked, Johnny. Bye. And your prostate too!"

"Bye, Ma."

"Bye."

I can't wait to get home to my wife!

Pulling into his driveway, he feels like an entire week has just passed. *I am so glad to be home!*

Walking through the front door, Oliver, the family beagle, greets him. *I love this dog. He's always happy to see me. I wonder where Sandra is.*

There was no sign of her or the kids as he passed the kitchen. *Maybe she's down the street at Martha's house again with the kids. I can't wait to tell her about my day and my great news.*

As he continues down the hallway, he pokes his head in the den. *Ah, there she is. I'm so glad she's home.*

"Sandra, you wouldn't believe the day I've had." John gives her a hug and a kiss on the cheek while she sits at her laptop. She is unresponsive. "Where are the kids?"

"My mom took them out for ice cream."

"How was your day?" John can see that his wife has already changed out of her work clothes and into her sweats.

"Look at this post on Facebook." It's as if she didn't even hear his question about her day. "Martin fell into the lady in front of him at the Clippers game."

"I called you."

"Oh, was that you? I ordered some pizza. You got any cash?"

Pizza again? Seriously?

"Yeah, I'll go wait for the pizza in the living room."

"Thanks."

John sits on the couch in the living room. He thinks to himself, *She doesn't even care that I'm home. She couldn't care less about what happened to me today. Might as well have stayed at work. Maybe I could still meet up with Stan and Christine.*

As John sits on the couch feeling lonely and frustrated waiting for the pizza, he begins to think about the events of his day and how his friends rallied around him. Then his mind wanders to Christine. *She is so thoughtful.*

Stop. Rewind. The story doesn't have to go like this. Let's change it up, shall we?

New and improved revised edition:

Say hello to happy, confident, and accomplished Mr. John Johnson. His life might be considered average, but for him it's exactly as he wants it to be, with a beautiful wife, three adorable kids, a house, a dog he loves, and two cars soon to be paid off. Our story begins with the sound of the 6:00 a.m. alarm. John rolls over to turn it off and then rolls back toward his wife, Sandra, feeling her naked body against his, and thinks, *Even in the morning she's stunningly beautiful.*

John jumps out of bed and into the shower. The shower door opens as Sandra enters to join him. [No details here. This scenario is rated PG. Use your imagination.]

As they towel off, they talk about the day ahead. "My mom wants to take the kids for ice cream after school, and she offered to keep them at her house for the night," Sandra says. "What do you think? We could go out or stay in."

John feels a surge of excitement. "I'd love to stay in. I love having the house to ourselves."

"Done," Sandra says. "I'll see if my mom wouldn't mind bringing them home in the morning."

"Hey, sweetie." John pauses. "There are rumors of layoffs again. I know I've had a good quarter, so I think I'm safe, but you never know."

"Really, again?" Sandra makes a face. "Just like the rumor about Christine being transferred because she 'couldn't handle the stress' last month. It's funny how people like to talk. I'm so glad you helped put all those rumors to rest. I would love to work with you—you always look out for the whole team and not just yourself."

"I'd better get dressed and get out of here if I'm going to leave on time tonight," John says as he playfully poses like a male bodybuilder. "Stop eyeing my body and let me get to work." They both laugh.

John finishes getting ready and gives Sandra a long kiss and hug goodbye. "I'll see you tonight. I love you."

Sandra smiles. "I love you more."

As John opens the door to his favorite routine coffee stop, he notices an attractive woman approaching, and he holds the door for her. John thinks, *I'll bet my wife would look good in that outfit. I can't wait to get home to my wife.*

As John approaches the counter to order his espresso, his cell phone rings. "Hey, Stan, what's the latest?"

"The latest is I'm getting fired, that's the latest. And you might be going too. What are you going to do?"

"Stan, chill, I'm gonna order my espresso, that's what I'm gonna do. Hold on."

John smiles and looks up at the barista. Noticing her bright purple bra peeking out from the top of her blouse, he focuses on his order. "Can I get a double espresso, please, and a triple zombie?"

John returns to his phone. "Stan, I just ordered you a zombie. Stop worrying—let's not play into the rumors. Bye, Stan. I'll see you soon." John hangs up with Stan and pays for his drinks. Then he puts two dollars in the tip jar and says, "Don't you hate the rude person who is on their phone when they should be ordering?"

The barista smiles and says, "Thank you."

With a coffee in each hand, John heads for his car. *I sure hope Stan is wrong*, he thinks, *but no matter what happens, I know Sandra will be home waiting for me. I can't wait to get home to my wife.*

John arrives at work, struts through the parking lot, and heads to the elevator. When the elevator door opens, he sees a woman bent over fixing her shoe. As she stands, he sees that it's Vanessa.

"Shoe problems?" John asks with a chuckle. "Hey, are you headed to Stan's office?"

"Yes, I am," Vanessa replies.

"Would you mind taking this to him?"

"Not at all. I'd be happy to."

John hands Vanessa the coffee. "Thanks," he says, and exits the elevator.

"Oh, wait," Vanessa calls. "Christine is looking for you. She says it's urgent."

John smiles. "Thanks for letting me know." The elevator door closes.

John reminisces about his morning with his wife. *I'm the luckiest guy in the world. I can't wait to get home to my wife.*

As he turns the corner, he hears whispers coming from the group of female employees gathered around Caroline, the company receptionist.

"Good morning, ladies." John stops at the counter. "What's the latest?"

Silence. Then Caroline says, "Christine needs to talk to you right away, Mr. Johnson."

As he walks away, he can hear whispers again. John sips his coffee and enters Christine's office. "Good morning," he says.

Christine stands, and John sees the high slit in her skirt running up the side of her leg. John bounces his eyes back to her eyes. "What's up?"

"John, I found out from Vanessa that you are being let go today."

"Really?"

"Yes, you know your three o'clock with Mr. Winlock? Well. . ."

"Well, I guess we'll find out at three. I hope it's just rumors again. Do you think it's true?"

"I think maybe, yeah. I mean, Vanessa thinks she heard something."

"Thanks for giving me a heads-up," John says.

"If I hear anything else, I'll let you know."

"Thank you." John sips his coffee and heads to his office but stops at Charlotte's desk first.

"Good morning, Charlotte." He notices she's looking very sharp and professional.

"Good morning, boss. Thank you for letting me leave early yesterday to see my mom."

"Of course. How is she?" John asks.

"Oh, so much better, thank you."

"Well, I'm glad she's doing better."

"I've added your three o'clock with Mr. Winlock to your calendar."

"Thank you, Charlotte."

John walks into his office and sits at his desk. *Could the rumors be true this time? Will I lose my job? Nah, they're probably just rumors.*

John taps his cell to call his wife. Sandra answers, "Hey, hot stuff." The sound of her voice cheers him instantly.

"Hey, beautiful, I can't wait for tonight. I miss you already."

"Me too. Have you heard anything?"

"Christine thinks the rumors might be true this time. She thinks I might be let go."

"John, I doubt it. You said you had a great quarter. If they let you go, that would be stupid. Try not to worry. No matter what, we'll work it out together. I'm behind you, honey. I know we'll be okay. Ah, I gotta go, I just spilled coffee on my white blouse. I love you."

"I love you too."

As he hangs up, he thinks, *I can't wait to get home to my wife.*

John jumps in and tackles the pile of messages on his desk.

Hours pass quickly.

Suddenly there's a knock on the door.

"Yes?"

Christine enters with Mary, Vanessa, Stan, and Stephanie close behind.

As they take a seat, Stephanie breaks the silence. "I did some digging. Mr. Winlock was given an ultimatum by the Dragon Lady. If numbers didn't rise by the third quarter, he had to let go of somebody. Maybe if you ask for another quarter to get numbers up, he'll reconsider."

John casually sits back in his chair. "I know Winlock. He'd never risk taking a chance, and I had a good quarter. What about you, Stan?"

"Eh," Stan says, "I'm safe. I ran into Rob in the parking lot."

Mary chimes in. "They really need help over at the Lincoln Park building. You could switch departments."

"I might be able to move things around in my department," Stan says.

"Thank you. I appreciate your concern, but I'll be okay."

"Either way," Stan says, trying to relieve some of the tension, "let's all meet up at McGee's tonight after work. You in, John?"

"No," John says, "I have plans with my wife. My awesome mother-in-law is taking the kids."

Christine says, "Well, we wouldn't want to mess with those plans."

"Have a great time," Stephanie says as all the ladies leave while Stan lags behind.

"Having hot pudding for supper, eh?" Stan says.

"Stan, enough," John replies. "You're just jealous."

"You know it," Stan agrees. "I haven't had any action since my wife—"

"Stan, yeah, I get it. Now get outta here so I can get some more work done, 'cause I'm out by five today."

"Ooookay, catch ya later." With that Stan heads out. "Hey, thanks for the coffee."

"You're welcome."

As Stan leaves, John thinks to himself, *I can't wait to get home to my wife.*

Wanting to head out by 5:00 p.m., John has no problem working through lunch.

And then, finally, it's time to head to his 3:00 appointment with Mr. Winlock. As he takes the elevator up a floor, he thinks about his wife and the amazing morning they had together.

"Mr. Winlock is waiting for you." Stephanie tries to smile but can't.

Whatever happens, I still get to go home to my awesome wife, John thinks as he walks through the door of Pete Winlock's office.

"John, sit down," Pete says. "I've been reviewing your files, and I'm promoting you to VP of operations."

Ha! John thinks. "Thank you."

"I'll brief you tomorrow. My kid's got another baseball game."

As John walks down the hall, headed back to his office, he thinks, *I can't wait to call my wife!*

Christine, Stan, Mary, and Vanessa follow John back into his office. John is smiling.

"What happened?" Christine demands.

"I got promoted to VP. Wait, hold on, I need to call my wife and tell her the news."

Sandra answers the phone. "Hey, babe! Do you know anything?"

"Yes," John says with a smirk. "You are now talking to the new VP of operations."

"What?! I'm so excited for you. Congratulations!"

Stan, Christine, Mary, and Vanessa start cheering in the background.

"What's going on?" Sandra asks.

John laughs. "Stan, Christine, Mary, and Vanessa are all in my office."

"Oh," Sandra says with delight. "I'm glad you have a cheer-leading crew."

"I love you, honey," John says, "I'll see you tonight."

"I love you," the rest of the gang all chant in unison while Sandra says, "I love you more, and I'm so proud of you."

As John hangs up the phone, Mary asks, "Does the Dragon Lady know?"

John chuckles. "I think she's the one who made it happen. Hey, thanks for the support, guys, but I have to get back to work. I'm not working late tonight. I have to get home to my wife."

As they leave, Stan says, "Did I tell you ladies about the dog with three legs. . . ?"

John gets back to work and at 4:00 p.m. decides to call it a day.

I am going home to my wife.

He passes Charlotte's desk. "Charlotte, I got a promotion today, so we may be moving up a floor. I'll let you know."

Charlotte says, "Congratulations, John, you deserve it."

"Thank you." John heads to the elevator quickly without stopping to talk to anyone.

On the ride home, John stops at a florist and gets his wife a dozen red roses. As he walks back to his car, he thinks, *I can't wait to get home to my wife.*

Back in his car, his phone rings.

"Hi, Ma."

"Hello, Johnny, it's Mom."

"Yeah, I know. I said, 'Hi, Ma.' "

John continues, "Mom, Evelyn has the kids tonight, so please don't call us."

"Johnny, why would I do that?"

"Mom, why would you stop by unannounced after your yoga class?"

"Johnny, a grandmother should be able to visit her grandkids whenever she wants."

"I was in my underwear, Mom, and the kids weren't even home."

"Oh yeah," his mom concedes, "they were at that church thing. Your kids are at church a lot."

"So please don't stop by or call tonight, okay?"

"Okay, honey. Are you still coming over this weekend?"

"Yes, Mom, Sandra said Sunday would work best."

"Oh good. We'll see you Sunday." He hears his mom yelling, "George, George, you'd better put that donut back! You heard what your doctor said." Then she comes back on the line. "Johnny, I've gotta go, your father is trying to eat a donut. I'll see you Sunday."

"Okay, Ma, see you Sunday. Love you."

"Love you, Johnny. Bye." He hears his mother's voice: "George, George, I'm gonna. . ." John laughs as he hangs up the phone.

John pulls into his driveway and feels a rush of energy and excitement. As he climbs out of the car, he sees his wife coming to greet him.

"You're home early!" Sandra says with delight.

John gives her a big hug and a kiss. Grabbing the flowers from the back seat, he hands them to her.

"Oh John, they're beautiful. I love them! Congratulations on your promotion. I'm so proud of you. I'm not at all surprised. You're going to be the best VP."

John walks arm in arm into his house with his pretty wife, feeling like a king.

The rest of the evening is delightful, erotic, and memorable, but this is where the story ends. PG, remember?

I know this is a silly question, but which story would you rather be living?

A wife who is attentive, loving, and available can massively alter a man's overall demeanor. When a man feels loved, respected, and adored, he's not looking for affection in other places. You don't have to drastically change your day to offer affirmations of love and value to your husband—you just need to be available for him. In the second story above, when John had someone in his corner, he was able to go through his day with confidence. When you are in your husband's corner and cheering for him, you enable him to soar.

Never Be Outplayed

My husband is a pastor, so I hear others' praises of him often. Most days he's surrounded by delightful and beautiful women—lovely women who offer respect and support. One day I walked into his office to clapping and cheers of praise. Literally. He had helped this group of attractive, kind, and attentive women, and they were showing appreciation by cheering for him. Seeing their outpouring of gratitude warmed my heart. Another time he was undergoing physical therapy and had to strut across the treatment area (doing a move that was part of his treatment), and many of the ladies present cheered him on. I was in the lobby writing, but he told me about the incident once we were in the car, and I was delighted to hear what had happened.

I'm thrilled these types of occasions aren't uncommon for him. But—and here's my point—I make a mental note of the occurrence and then think to myself, *Bring it on!* I accept the challenge from others to love my husband *better*. Not in a contentious way, but in a way that causes me to check myself and *my* actions toward him. If he's getting cheered for at work and I'm on him because the trash didn't go out, how do you think that's going to play out in his affections toward me?

Continually be looking for ways to express your appreciation of your husband as a man. It can be as simple as saying thank you or noticing an admirable quality about him. And don't underplay his physical needs. In *The Five Love Languages* Dr. Gary Chapman explains that sexual desire is a physical thing for a man and is connected to the seminal vesicles and the buildup of sperm. When the sperm builds up and the seminal vessels are full, the body pushes for release.[1]

As his wife, how do you want this release to happen?

My friend and fellow pastor's wife, Nichole, when asked what her role is in her husband's ministry, says, "My ministry is to have sex with the pastor, and there's no delegating it." She understands the importance of a husband not falling prey to the schemes of the evil one. Satan's mission is to steal and destroy and separate families. First Corinthians 7:5 tells us, "Stop depriving one another, except by agreement for a time, so that you may devote yourselves to prayer, and come together again so that Satan will not tempt you because of your lack of self-control."

You are the only one who can meet your husband's needs physically. That, my sweet friend, usually trumps anything else. It's kind of like the game of chess. The queen, which stands right next to the king, is the most powerful piece on the board. You are the queen. You are the best and most important "piece" in his life. You have the ability to build him up or tear him down. Always be looking for ways to appreciate him that will outshine all the sexual images and female cheerleaders surrounding him. I would rather live with a man who is continually built up and feels like a king than with one who feels beaten up and worn down, and I'm sure you feel the same way. Not to mention one who is smiling.

Never, never, never allow another woman—or any other person, for that matter—to treat your husband better than you do. If you've married a wonderful man, as I hope you have, then he's receiving praise and accolades from others, many of them women. This you can count on.

Your "joint sessions of Congress" will be affected by how you treat each other all day long—day in and day out. It's how you appreciate each other and love each other *out* of the bedroom that will determine the health of your rendezvous *in* the bedroom. Make a habit of always treating your spouse well.

WHAT HE WANTS YOU TO KNOW:

"Please don't forget about me. Please remember me and my needs. I wish my wife would think of me more, especially with regard to intimacy."
—Andy, neglected husband

Praise in Action

"Mom, Dad's home!" I'd run outside only to find my kids were messing with me. So I'd go back to what I was doing. "Mom, Dad's home!" I'd run outside again only to find my kids were making sport of me again and entertaining the neighbors. This went on for. . .well, I really don't want to tell you, but for the sake of keeping some of my dignity intact, let's say three more times, but truthfully, it was more like seven or eight. I lost count.

My kids cracked themselves up, and I have to admit, their ploy cracked me up too. Not only did it get us all laughing, but it taught my kids something. They knew, and still know, that their mom is overjoyed by their dad's presence.

Years ago I heard a sermon with a story illustration about a little dog that had gotten lost and was trying to find his way home. This little pup got chased by a raccoon, got stuck in a fence, fell into a ditch, almost got captured by animal rescue, and after miles of running and searching, finally found his way back into the welcoming arms of his owner. Wrapping up the story, the pastor said, "Ladies, that is how we husbands feel after a long day. We long to get home to our wives."

I never forgot that story, and it prompted me to make a decision to greet my husband with enthusiasm daily, usually by booking it outside when I see his car. It's not hard to do because I am usually genuinely happy to see him—but even if I wasn't, I'd still greet him. Only good can come from a warm welcome.

Treat your husband like he is the man of your dreams, the man who will slay dragons for you, catch a bullet in his teeth, leap tall buildings. . .Yes, I know, I'm getting carried away here, but you get the idea. Offer unselfish adoration and respect and see if he doesn't become as close to all of those metaphors as any man can. Not because you are trying to "get something," but because he is *your* man. You are his wife and *that* is a high calling.

Make a habit of finding ways to show your husband physically and emotionally that you appreciate him, admire him, adore him, and choose him every day above all others. And remember, you can't "delegate" that, nor would you want to.

SECRET SEX MISSION #7

This is your mission if you wish to accept it: For the next two weeks, greet your husband with all the enthusiasm you can muster when he arrives home, or when you arrive home if he beats you there. Go outside when his car pulls up or wait outside for him. At the very least, meet him at the door. See how it affects your relationship. See what it does to your sex life.

ASK HIM

To piggyback on the idea in chapter 3 of giving your husband a clicker for a day and asking him to click every time he thinks about sex, enhance your intimacy by discussing the following questions. How often does he think about you? How often does he think about having sex with you? How often does he desire to *have* sex with you? Accept his answers as information you can use to make your marriage—and your adult nap time—better.

CHAPTER 8

MEN ARE VISUAL

> NOT TONIGHT, HONEY—
> I WENT SWIMSUIT SHOPPING, AND NOW I'M DEPRESSED.

I distinctly remember the day my husband threw away his *Playboy* magazines. He walked out the front door of our condo, rode down the elevator, then walked through the carport to the end of the driveway and tossed away years' worth of his stash. He had to make multiple trips. *Multiple.* Each trip carrying a stack of magazines.

You may be wondering if I was the one who prompted him to toss his collection. No, I wasn't. In fact, I had never said a word to him about it, not that day nor any day prior. And he didn't say a word to me about it either—he just gave me a ticket for a front-row seat to the *Playboy* toss matinee. Nonetheless, I'm quite certain I know why he made such a decision—it was because we had both made commitments to follow Jesus Christ shortly before, and this was an act of love. And one I got to watch.

I never held his magazines against him.

I understood something very critical about him then, and even more so now: men are visual. God made him that way; he is that way by God's design. The Bible tells us, "He [God] created them male and female, and He blessed them and named them Man in the day when they were created" (Genesis 5:2). Two completely different genders.

WHAT HE WANTS YOU TO KNOW:

"Please understand, men are visual; we notice attractive women."

—Neil, adoring husband

Men were formed with a built-in ignition switch with adrenaline-charged pleasure sensors called eyes. His eyes are distracted by beautiful shiny things called women—in multiple shapes and sizes. Whether they are curvy, round, smooth, pointed, his brain sends off a surge of pleasure. It's like a blast of crack cocaine—visual images can be euphoric for him. At this point, he has a choice: he can indulge his eyes, keep gazing, and allow his mind to wander, or he can bounce his eyes. But seriously, can we really beat him up over a second look now and then?

On NBC's *Seinfeld*, Jerry says to George, "Looking at cleavage is like looking at the sun. You don't stare at it. It's too risky. You get a sense of it, then you look away."[1]

In their book *Every Young Man's Battle*, Stephen Arterburn and Fred Stoeker relay an enlightening account that can give us more insight into men's visual nature. Pastor Jack Hayford was speaking at a conference where he told a story to thousands of men of how he had to either purify his mind and focus completely on God or masturbate in his car after a transaction with a pretty bank teller.[2]

Again, crack cocaine. Imagine that M&M's—or Skittles, whichever you prefer—were being randomly thrown in your mouth throughout the day. How many of these candies would you resist, and how many would you indulge in? Only the electrical jolt he gets is stronger than any M&M, and he's preprogrammed to react. It's like he's getting pleasure hits throughout his day. A shot here, a shot there.

Use the differences between male and female to make your marriage better. Unite as a team and work alongside him, using his heightened delight in what he sees to improve your sex life. Instead of leaving him tempted to tickle his eyes, my suggestion is for *you* to give him something to look at.

My beautiful friend Susan knows how to capitalize on her assets to keep her husband enticed. Knowing her husband was in the family room, she ran down the stairs, turned the corner, sauntered in front of him, pulled up her shirt, and flashed him her bare breasts. After her shirt went up, to her horror, she saw her father sitting directly behind her husband. Dad was seated at the kitchen table and had a second-row seat to the show. Mortified, she dove into the couch, where she buried her face. She said she curled up in a ball for what seemed like an eternity, thinking she'd never be able to look at her father again. Finally, she heard her dad say, "Little girl," even though she was forty-five years old at the time, "you've got to come into the kitchen at some point."

Great heart, bad execution. But you gotta give her credit for the effort. It's like when all the kids get participation trophies: they played but they knew they didn't really win anything.

But I'm the last person to judge her on this.

One day I wanted to model my new bra for my husband. The kids weren't due home for hours, so I decided it was a good time to parade my sexy new bra for him. After the fashion show, still shirtless, I went into the kitchen and started prepping for dinner. I had intended to go into our bedroom and put on a shirt, I really had, but I got distracted. The front door flung open, and before I could react, in walked my then twenty-three-year-old daughter with her friend. I was trapped in the kitchen as they stood and stared at me with bugged-out eyes. I can't tell you who was more shocked—me or the startled young ladies.

"Oh, I am so sorry!" I managed to say. My husband listened, very amused, wondering how I was going to explain this one. "I was just showing him my new. . .umm. . .oh, I am so sorry."

"It's okay," my daughter's friend Christine said without even a hint of a giggle, "you're married. It's okay."

My daughter laughed as I excused myself and ran past the girls to put on a shirt. Thank goodness she wasn't with one of her guy friends!

Living with Men

I've always found men to be captivating. Even when I was a little girl, while all the women gathered to talk, I was with my dad and the other men, listening, watching, taking in all they said and did. Guys are vastly different from us girls, and I'm fascinated by trying to get a handle on the way they think and feel.

For much of this chapter, I'm letting the men speak because, well, they're men. These forthcoming husbands have offered up sincere thoughts and feelings with honesty and candor. We can use this information, embrace the Wolverine in our men, and capitalize on their maleness to set our relationships on fire.

Please put previous notions aside and open your mind and heart in a way that can benefit your marriage. Receive these men's thoughts as merely helpful information to give you ideas for improving your own relationship with your husband.

WHAT HE WANTS YOU TO KNOW:

"I get tired of seeing you in the same dumpy old clothes without makeup. Understand, I love you, and your old dumpy clothes, and I think you're beautiful with or without makeup, but I'd also like you to 'clean up' for me from time to time.

"It's like when I fixed up my old barn with my grandpa. We fixed the bad places, slapped a coat of paint on it, and it looked really nice. I didn't love it any more, I didn't love it any less, but when people looked at it I smiled a little bit more and said, 'Yeah, that's mine.' I was just a bit prouder of it when it was 'prettied up.'

"When guys say physical appearance matters, I really don't think they mean you have to have a perfect drop-dead model look. But the one thing all those models have in common is that they take care of themselves. You can't expect someone to take pride in your appearance if you don't take pride in yourself first.

"There are plenty of women on TV and in magazines who do not have the perfect figure but are *smoking* hot. They keep up their physical appearance and 'put a coat of paint on the barn.' "

—Patrick, madly in love husband

In his book *The Secrets Men Keep*, Stephen Arterburn writes that a survey of 3,600 male respondents revealed that men care greatly about the appearance of their wives or significant others. Although these men felt free to answer honestly in an anonymous survey, the idea of broaching the subject with their wives was unthinkable. In fact, Arterburn said they'd "rather ride a pogo stick through an abandoned minefield."[3]

Struggle

I gained more and more weight with the births of each of my

children, fifty, then sixty, then upwards of seventy pounds. I felt like a whale stuck on the sand, unable to get back in the water, while continually gazing at the ocean and the life that could be. During this period, intimacy was difficult. I had to put ugly feelings aside and remind myself that I was still married and that I still—surprisingly so—had a husband who wanted this whale of a body. In fact, it didn't slow him down in the least. He still wanted to "try new things" and keep up our normal "playtime" schedule. I was disgusted by my appearance, tired from the demands of being a mom, and not feeling amorous in the least. I set out on a mission to get back in shape and return to my beach-ready body—but mostly I just wanted to feel better about myself. I began walking more than driving. I'd walk all around our neighborhood, walking to pick up my kids from school and any activity I could walk to, and I also began exercising daily.

A fun-loving friend said, "I see you walking everywhere, but your butt doesn't seem to be getting any smaller."

Not taking offense, I said, "I know, right?"

The struggle was real. My friend's quip was her way of offering sympathy. She understood my plight. I stayed in my pregnancy clothes for close to a year. My husband would often offer to take me shopping, but I'd give excuses with the trump card of "I'm going to lose weight, so there's no reason to buy clothes now."

Then as I finally did begin to lose weight, I'd pull out my old shabby clothes. Mike would take me out and try to buy me new outfits. I'd try things on and say, "Nothing worked," but secretly I was thinking we could use the funds for more important things, like the kids. It was hard for me to use family funds on myself. This frustrated my husband, but I didn't understand why. *Why does it matter to him so much? I mean, he knows the kids need things. I'm fine—I don't need anything.* He'd try to get me to the mall every chance he got, and it was the catalyst for many fights, whether we actually made it to the mall or not.

I didn't feel good about myself, and I didn't give much attention to my appearance other than trying to get back in shape. On the rare occasions I would "fancy up," Mike seemed to treat me better, and I'd feel anger and resentment toward him. Why would he treat me better when I looked better? Feeling frustrated, I asked him one day, "Why do you treat me differently based on the way I look?"

I wasn't ready for his answer: "You act differently when you look better."

The person who was changing their behavior was me, not him. I acted differently toward him, and he was merely responding.

The biggest change happened one day when I was working out and had a sudden epiphany: *Why I am spending so much time on my body only to put shabby, unattractive clothes on it?*

Maybe my body wasn't where I wanted it yet, but I wasn't helping myself by wearing clothes that didn't flatter me. The next time Mike took me shopping, I "miraculously" found some clothes that worked. I'm telling you, the man was so happy, you would have thought he had just purchased a new sports car! It gave our marriage a boost. Who knew I could have been making my marriage better with this one small change? Slowly, I began to take more care with my appearance, which was another boost for my marriage.

When I felt better about myself, I was more daring as a wife. My confidence increased, and I was more comfortable taking risks with my sexuality—letting that side out a little more. Our relationship ramped up from a "sports car" to a "romantic beach house."

Receiving and accepting my husband's input with regard to fashion and my overall appearance improved our marriage in a way I never thought possible. To date one of his favorite activities is to take me shopping—for shoes, clothes, makeup—anything I ask for. Sometimes surprise packages show up in the mail or I'll be getting ready to go to an event and a new dress will be sitting out for me.

I finally came to the realization that investing in myself—and my sexuality—was investing in my marriage. The bigger the investment, the bigger the payoff.

It was around this time that I began to understand how strongly a man is affected by what he sees and how I could use this fact to ramp up my marriage.

WHAT HE WANTS YOU TO KNOW:

"I want to be more than just roommates. I know you've gained weight over the years, but that doesn't change my love for you. I was so attracted to you when we first started dating back then; you always took care of yourself. But now you pull yourself out of bed in the morning, throw on some sweats and a big T-shirt, and stay that way for the rest of the day. You don't give me a reason to take a second look."

—Larry, reminiscent husband

While I was visiting one of my married girlfriends, somehow we got on the subject of underwear. She told me her underclothing was old and ratty. I distinctly remember her saying, "It doesn't matter. Nobody sees them anyway."

I felt sad to hear this, because the most important person sees that ratty underclothing. Unless maybe she literally meant *nobody*, and that's even sadder.

In her book *Is That All He Thinks About?* Marla Taviano encourages wives to "dump the frump." No matter what you weigh, pretty underwear and lingerie are available in your size. What we choose to put on our bodies will influence our sense of self. When we look drab and dowdy, do we really still expect our husbands to romance us? Dump the granny panties, tattered bras, and grungy sweats, and make a little effort to look good, because "sexy is as sexy does." The better you look, the better you'll feel.[4]

WHAT HE WANTS YOU TO KNOW:

"I'm attracted to you both physically and relationally. When it comes to physical attractiveness, I think you look great all dressed up or in sweatpants and a T-shirt. If there's an increased attraction to you when you're dressed up, it's not because of how you look but because of the likely implication of how you feel.

"When you've had a busy day, running around with the kids or doing more work around the house, and you're not made up, and you're obviously tired, I still think you look great—and I mean that!—but that also means you likely have less confidence in yourself physically.

"So when you're made up a little, and I'm not talking all kinds of dressed up, it likely implies that you're feeling more balanced, and that will show. When you feel good about yourself and are confident, that will get expressed in your appearance, sometimes even subconsciously."

—Ronald, conscientious husband

"I think you are beautiful. I appreciate the way you eat healthy and exercise on a consistent basis. I love your style and your ability to dress modestly but fashionably. However, what makes me more attracted to you physically is your own inner confidence. Nothing is sexier than confidence.

"On the other hand, a big turnoff would be insecurity. Nothing would be more frustrating than telling you how beautiful you are only to hear you say that you aren't. It would be like my thoughts and words don't matter because of your own insecurity. Confidence is key. I think you are super attractive, and your confidence makes you even more attractive."

—Ashton, proud husband

Can I be blunt? No one wants to be married to someone who has "let it all go." Not just because of how we would look, but because our lack of self-care would reveal how poorly we felt about ourselves. I'm not talking about having plastic surgery or losing weight; I'm talking about caring for the goods we have.

The antidote to insecurity is confidence. We can be confident at any size, at any age, and in any season.

In *The Secrets Men Keep* Stephen Arterburn talks about some of the justifications women give when a husband becomes brave enough to bring up his wife's appearance. She might say, "It's the inside that matters," or "Why can't you love me for who I am?" or "Lose weight and clean up your act before you criticize me." He says responses like these may cause an internal struggle within men or prompt them to withdraw. For many of the men

Arterburn surveyed, the bottom line was that they wouldn't now propose to the woman they were currently married to—based mostly on her appearance.[5] You can see how these conflicting feelings could cause major marriage problems.

If you fear your husband might be less than captivated by your present appearance, you can turn the situation around right now by being understanding and willing to make a few tweaks. Not huge tweaks, mind you, but little changes that will bring about huge marital payouts.

The Bible implores us to live with each other in an understanding way. "To sum up, all of you be harmonious, sympathetic, brotherly, kindhearted, and humble in spirit; not returning evil for evil or insult for insult, but giving a blessing instead; for you were called for the very purpose that you might inherit a blessing" (1 Peter 3:8–9).

WHAT HE WANTS YOU TO KNOW:

"It makes me feel good when you look good. I guess you could say it is the curse of men being visual. When you take care of yourself, it helps me to know that I am taking care of you. As a man I am proud to show you off; when you are dressed up, my attraction to you increases. . . . That's just the honest truth."

—Carlos, giddy husband

> "I want you to take care of yourself. It matters to me that you make an effort to look good. If you don't take care of yourself and make no effort to look good, then it makes me think you don't believe me when I tell you you're beautiful, and it shows me you don't care if I'm attracted to you or not.
>
> "When you make the effort to look good, it shows me you appreciate me, care about me, and want me to be attracted to you, which communicates you're attracted to me."
>
> —Byron, committed husband

A friend of mine went away for a weekend for a family wedding. Her husband had to stay behind but decided when she arrived home, he'd surprise her with the new closet he knew she wanted. To throw her off, he acted like his back was out and he couldn't get off the couch. He worked hard all weekend building her the new closet she had been asking for. He went at it like he was building the Taj Mahal—total focus; nothing else mattered; he was on a mission to surprise his wife. When she arrived home, she was absolutely touched and delighted. What would make a husband go to these lengths to surprise his wife and work tirelessly on a project that he quite frankly didn't care much about either way? She pays attention to his needs and desires, and he pays attention to her needs and desires. Who started this cycle? Does it matter?

In his book *Sheet Music*, Dr. Kevin Leman writes, "If a man is home-centered—in large part because at home he feels like he's loved, wanted, and accepted for who he is, and he has a wife who wants to please him—he'll do anything that will strengthen the home because that's his most important world."[6]

Pulling It All Together

Let me put it this way: What if your husband stopped talking to you? What if he spent much of his time home on the couch playing video games and belching? And what if he stopped giving you hugs and never said anything complimentary? Would you be attracted to him even if he had a rad bod? We women like to communicate and to feel understood and valued. None of the men who provided the "Anonymous Husband" quotes throughout this book said, "I wish my wife would talk to me more." Not one. In fact, I don't think I've ever heard a man say that.

He likes to look at you.

In light of the insights we've learned from the anonymous husbands quoted within these pages, instead of condemning our men for how they are wired, let's go with it and use what we've learned to make our marriages better. When your husband compliments your physique, accept his praises and use his words to boost your confidence.

Be mindful daily of what you are feeding his eyes. Many wives are concerned about what their husbands are eating—and rightly so, because we want them to be healthy—but we should be just as concerned with what their eyes are filling up with. We've all heard the advice that a man should marry a woman who's a good cook. I say, you can learn how to cook or order in great food, but a woman who fills her husband's eyes is a wise woman. I even have a verse to support this idea: "The wise woman builds her house, but the foolish tears it down with her own hands" (Proverbs 14:1). A little cheesy, I know, but I'm just trying to make a point here.

Think about what your husband sees on a day-to-day basis.

Are you giving his eyes something tantalizing? Are you giving him a reason to want to come home? We don't know what images our men may have encountered throughout their day. I would prefer that my husband get his fill from looking at me. Don't you feel the same?

We women may have trouble understanding men's visual nature because we tend to be stimulated more by words, touch, and acts of kindness. Our husbands are undeniably hugely stimulated by what they see. Instead of resenting or resisting this fact, have fun with it. You'll be surprised by how happy you can make him with a little flash of something enticing, and you'll feel more chase-worthy. Catching his eye and experiencing his reactions to your appeal will boost your confidence, build his enthusiasm for you, and create anticipation for both of you. Anticipation, in turn, will accelerate your desire and craving for him.

Don't starve his eyes. When you have a full stomach, you are way less tempted by Boston cream pie. He loves to see as much of you as he can. Help him to stay away from Boston cream pie by keeping his eyes full.

Some Fun Ways to Fill His Eyes
- Flaunt confidence. Strut your stuff like you are the beauty he knows you are. Tease him. Enjoy the fun of being female.
- When you're passing him, flash a little—ahem, whatever you want—and just keep moving. When our kids are over and I leave the room and notice that I've caught my husband's eye, I will flash him and keep walking down the hallway. Sorry, kids, now you know.
- Want him to pitch the remote? Be the best show on late night.

- Keep a supply of sexy lingerie. I've heard it said that what matters most is what it looks like on the floor because it doesn't stay on long. I totally disagree. When it doesn't feel good on, you are less likely to put it on. The best tip I have when purchasing lingerie is to make sure it feels good on, that you feel good about yourself in it, and that you're comfortable wearing it. Stock up on comfy sexy stuff. It can be as simple as a see-through shirt.
- Bend over in front of him as often as possible. And don't forget to lift your shirt now and then.
- Unbutton your shirt one button every three minutes and see how long it takes him to notice.
- Walk around in your underclothing for a while before getting dressed.
- Dress in front of him. I've heard of women dressing in their closets. Please step out of the closet.
- Undress in front of him. It goes like this: "Honey, I'm going to go change if you want to come watch." Trust me, he'll appreciate the invitation.
- Keep the lights on when you're churning butter.
- Give him a say in your appearance. Make purchases based on his preferences.
- Offer him license to request outfits he likes to see you in.
- Have an "accidental" *Oops! I lost my [whatever]* moment.

Add your own and please send them to me at my website, LuSays.com. I'd love to hear from you and add to the list.

To wrap it all up, your husband wants you to feel sexy, and he wants to be drawn in by your sensuousness. It's okay—remember, you're married.

SECRET SEX MISSION #8

This is your mission if you wish to accept it: Start checking off items on the list above by testing them out. Keep going until the entire list has been checked. Come up with some fun ideas of your own. See if it doesn't take your horizontal tango to a hotter foxtrot.

ASK HIM

Open up a discussion about what he prefers to see you wearing. Ask him to go shopping with you, and let him offer input about your overall appearance.

CHAPTER 9

WHEN HIS ENGINE IS ON IDLE OR YOU WANT TO REV THINGS UP

> MAYBE TONIGHT, HONEY—
> MAYBE?

"Josh has a very high libido. He can be suffering with the flu, be sleep deprived, have his legs severed, his eyes gouged out, and still be ready for sex."

—Rachel, tired wife

This quote exemplifies the typical conception about men and their sexual appetite. The idea is that men just never say no, but that's simply not true. The reason many women never hear no is because their men are left wanting. On the other hand, if he is saying no from time to time, it doesn't necessarily mean something is wrong. Men do turn down sex occasionally, especially when they have a wife who is an eager participant. It's like eating chocolate chip cookies: when you know you can eat them whenever you want, sometimes you'll save some for later. Having said that, some of you can't remember the last time you had some "chocolate chip cookies," or you do remember, and it was way too long ago.

My dear sister, if he doesn't seem interested in sex, you most likely are feeling unloved, undesired, and inadequate. How I wish

I could sit down with you over a cup of coffee and hear your story. My heart cries for you and your marriage. You know this is not what you envisioned for your marriage, and you know it's not what God intends.

My goal is to help you have the sexual relationship that God intends for marriage and that you so desperately crave. Oftentimes, slight course changes can reap huge results.

Please stop for a moment and pray. Ask God to give you an open heart to hear what you can do, or possibly stop doing, to help your husband in this area. Allow God to speak to you.

Now, before we move on, I'd like to applaud you for reading a book like this one. It shows your commitment to nurturing a richer, more fruitful, more passionate marriage. Please receive this information with an open heart and a determination to usher in a new steam-filled future. You may read something here, try it out, and—*bingo!*—all adult fun is back on track. I have received reports from women who have taken the steps I'm about to share with you, and almost magically, whatever the issue was, it vanished. I'm praying yours is the next report.

As you are most likely already aware, sometimes revving things up in the bedroom takes a bit more work. If there was something you could do to help generate within your husband a greater interest in sex, even if it was emotionally taxing, wouldn't it be worth giving it a try? Please don't try a few things and then give up, thinking you've "done all you can." It is going to take work. It is going to take time. It is going to take consistency. But I guarantee it will be worth your efforts. Don't give up. Every step you take is a step closer to the marriage of your dreams.

In most cases an absence of sex in a marriage is a symptom of a bigger problem, and solving it takes teamwork. You'll need an atmosphere of trust and safety. Collaboration is essential to keep things rocking, but he may be embarrassed to talk about any problems. How you respond will determine how open and vulnerable he will be.

There are many different reasons your husband may not be interested in sex. Because each situation is unique, no one answer or solution will help every couple. You'll need to lean on God more than ever as you flush out the reasons for the lack of hanky-panky in your marriage. You will need patience and steadfastness. Do your best to stay focused on the goal—the prize of a more intimate relationship.

Being in a sexless or near-sexless marriage is such a lonely problem to have. You can't just sit around over tea with your girlfriends and have a discussion about why your husband seems to have no desire to touch you anymore.

And you can be certain he's not going to appeal to his buddies in the locker room. "Hey, guys, I haven't had sex in weeks, no, make that months—actually, I think it's been years. Can we all go for lunch and talk about it?" Frankly, the problem of sexless marriages is more common than most realize. We don't hear about it because it is often too embarrassing and painful to talk about. And most likely more for him than for you.

Perhaps you have separate lives that don't seem to intersect long enough for sexual trysts. Your life paths have veered off in separate directions, and now you've decided it's time for a course change and you're determined to get back on the same track. Feeling like you are doing life alone when you're married is indeed painfully lonely.

Along with your feelings of loneliness, certain fears may have surfaced. So let's address what you might already be thinking. Here are some common fears women may have:

- *He's into pornography.* This really is a scary thought. So scary you don't even want to ask him. But if this is the case, and he is into porn, it needs to be addressed. It probably is not the case, but don't be afraid to ask the tough questions. If he admits it or you know it to be true, *do not* overreact. Be understanding. Talk with him and find out why he is choosing videos/computer screens/fake women over you. Listen without judgment. Assure him he does not need to make that choice anymore and let him know you are available sexually. That simple conversation may resolve this problem or at least set you on the road to success. If the problem goes deeper, don't hesitate to reach out for help. Know you are not alone. Many women are struggling—just like you—to navigate such a tough dilemma. Most importantly, realize that this is an "us" problem, not a "him" problem. Tackle it together. With no judgment. Great resources are available to help you (see the resource list at the back of this book).
- *He's having an affair.* He probably is not, but you might be thinking it from time to time. Don't allow your mind to run wild. Some men have a lower sex drive than others. Some men have lower testosterone levels. Your husband may be one of those men.
- *He's self-gratifying.* Some men fly solo so often that they lose desire for intimacy with a person. The likelihood that this is your situation is rare, but again, you need to ask the tough questions. If you find out why, you can take steps to fix the problem. Be brave and be willing to feel uncomfortable in order to uncover the real issues. This problem may be something you can fix together, or both of you may need to get help resolving it. If this is your

situation, please refrain from judgment, be understanding, and focus on the end goal.

- *I'm not desirable.* You're wondering, *Is something wrong with me? Am I not attractive enough? Does he think I'm too thin? Too fat? Too [you fill in the blank]?* Put your worries to rest. This is probably not the case. Share your concerns with your husband and be willing to understand his perspective. Most likely he is still madly in love with you and feels attracted to you. Nonetheless, ask him outright and give him a safe space to talk about his feelings.

- *Something is terribly wrong with him.* If a medical issue is the problem, it needs to be addressed. Erectile dysfunction and heart disease can be linked. This indeed is an extremely sensitive conversation. Tread lightly, but a suggestion to see a doctor for a physical might be in order. He may have a medical problem, and if that's the case, a doctor is what you need. The principles in this chapter are good for your marriage, but if something is physically wrong, only medical help will work.

If you are struggling with an absence of sex in your marriage, you are not alone! Listen to what some other wives have to say about their own dry spells from horizontal refreshments:

> "I have been turned down a whole lot! I feel very angry and upset and frustrated. Why? He has stupid excuses. Sometimes I feel like I don't care anymore. It makes me feel distant. I don't want him touching me or hugging me because it makes me feel turned on and I don't want to feel turned on and then be rejected. Makes me not care anymore. I feel angry."
>
> —Sue, angry wife

"I've been turned down quite a bit. It makes me feel unattractive, overweight, unwanted, unloved, lonely, and all around horrible! It makes me even *more* insecure!"

—Patty, insecure wife

"There is nothing worse than lying in bed next to a man who doesn't want you."

—Lana, hopeless wife

"When I was turned down for sex, it made me feel undesirable. I wondered if there was something wrong with me or if he was into porn or had a wandering heart. However, once we actually *talked* about it—instead of me keeping it in—he realized he had been distracted and absorbed by work and school. It was scary to talk about it because I didn't want to feel more rejected than I already felt. We now make it a point to have romantic date nights and voice what we desire sexually. I recently learned what he finds sexy, which I never would have known had we not opened up communication about sex. But now we have been intimate more than I want to, which is a refreshing change."

—Andrea, rejuvenated wife

Focusing on the Prize

Are you ready to get to work on finding solutions? Think of this challenge as a "we" problem, not a "he" problem, and keep a narrow focus on your goal, considering your overall relationship. Sex is extremely intimate, leaving us vulnerable and exposed. Our partners need to be able to trust us. Have the courage to examine yourself to rule out possible actions that may have contributed, or continue to contribute, to his idling engine.

Dealing with Anger

Feeling angry when you find yourself in this "wanting" situation is completely understandable and expected. Nonetheless, anger is your enemy. This may be the most difficult step, but to make progress, you must keep angry emotions in check. Being mad at him will only push him further away, when what he really needs right now is your understanding. If you've displayed irritation with him, my guess is that it hasn't gotten you any closer to mattress dancing. As painful as it may be for you, try to look at things from his perspective.

Asking Tough Questions about Him and Taking Inventory

Let's talk about testosterone. It's one of the first stops when dealing with a man who seems blasé about dancing in the sheets. Testosterone levels, which decrease as a man ages, can affect a man's sex drive. It's possible that what you are experiencing is a natural part of aging. But if his aging has ushered in a complete disinterest in gettin' jiggy with it, that is indeed not normal. A visit to a doctor can determine if low testosterone levels are your culprit. Keep in mind that his testosterone levels are usually highest in the morning, so you may want to get dancing with that intel.

Factors that can affect his sex drive are stress, depression, grief, and feelings of inadequacy. If any of the above are the cause, he needs support, sympathy, and patience to help him deal with such strong deterrents. Has he had what he considers a huge failure recently? Bottled-up inadequacy can spill over into the bedroom.

Medications also can decrease sex drive and cause erectile dysfunction. It could take him longer to "jump to," and how you respond can affect how an intimate encounter plays out. Be careful not to add to his feelings of inadequacy in any way if this happens.

When we add up aging, internal and external pressures, and medications, we begin to paint a picture of what might be going on.

Bob Berkowitz, PhD, and Susan Yager-Berkowitz, in their book *He's Just Not Up for It Anymore*, report that a small percentage of men with erectile dysfunction—roughly only 20 percent—consult a professional for help. Many men can be ready to go almost instantly, but as a man ages he may need more stimulation, which is not uncommon. Studies have shown that men over the age of forty tend to experience a decline in the way they function sexually. It has been reported that over 30 million men in the United States have trouble with ED, and that just includes the reported accounts.[1]

When you think about all the ads and commercials for Viagra, Cialis, and Levitra, you know it's more common than most talk about. With this in mind, consider that your husband may be embarrassed about his inability to maintain an erection, and he may just find it easier to avoid you than engage in marital congress. Sometimes the solution is more cooperation "in the ring," working with his body and enjoying each other no matter what happens. Or doesn't happen. Most, if not all, men will struggle with ED at some point in their lives. How a wife handles these occurrences will determine her husband's level of embarrassment. Ideally no embarrassment or shame is the goal. And above all, don't take any sexual dysfunction personally. As in *There must be something wrong with me. I'm not pretty enough, thin enough, sexy enough. . . .* And so on. Don't allow yourself to go down that dark path. It will only add to his already bruised ego, and it will not help your plight in the least.

If in the middle of boom-boom Charlie takes a nap, he needs

to be able to say, "I don't know what happened, but I need a little help here." The smart wife will turn this kind of invitation into more fun.

Do your best to look beyond yourself and take action steps to turn things around. Use the "slow times" to explore new ways to enhance your "tumbling" and enjoy spending time together. If his body absolutely refuses to cooperate, move on when he's ready to. And don't bring it up later—unless *he* wants to talk about it. Anytime he has trouble in the bedroom, and it didn't end well, initiate another rendezvous as soon as possible, preferably the next day. You want him back on the horse quickly and not thinking about a not-so-enjoyable encounter.

Asking Yourself Some Tough Questions

Have you hurt his feelings? That question may make it seem as if you are dealing with a five-year-old girl, but men are way more sensitive than most women understand. "As big and tough as men appear on the outside, they're really little boys on the inside. The entire male species is extremely susceptible to criticism," writes Dr. Kevin Leman in *Under the Sheets*.[2]

Yes, men can get their feelings hurt, especially by the women they desire to please the most. A wife holds a very critical piece of a man's heart. His feelings as a man are greatly influenced by you, his wife. If you have unintentionally said something that was hurtful or demeaning or overcritical, it may have blocked his "performance mechanism." Maybe? The good news is that you can unblock it with affirming words.

Have you *talked* (revealed a bit too much about adult play-time) to your friends? You may think a simple conversation with your girlfriend will stay between you and her, but never forget that if she has a husband, she could very well tell him. And he in turn may say something to *your* husband. Words have a way of surfacing. It is never okay to divulge intimate details about your sex life with your friends, even close friends. If your husband thinks you are doing this, it could cause him to shut down and not trust you. Never discuss intimate encounters between you and your spouse with others, unless it's something you want to get back to him. The bedroom is sacred, and what happens there needs to stay there.

The only exception to this is if you are going to someone you trust for counsel. However, even then be selective about the words you choose and the person you choose.

Is it possible that something that happened in the bedroom embarrassed him? Did you expose something he may be sensitive about? A man can be self-conscious about his body or insecure about "performance." Be careful to use only positive words in regard to your "playtime." Again, think back on Dr. Leman's words: "As big and tough as men appear on the outside, they're really little boys on the inside."[3]

WHAT HE WANTS YOU TO KNOW:

"I don't want to disappoint you or let you down or ever feel like I'm not good enough."

—Hank, hesitant husband

If he thinks he is going to fail with you, he may not even try; it is just way too risky for him. He can fail at work. He can fail on the racquetball court. He can fail in friendship. He can fail with investments. But the one place your husband *always* needs to hit a home run is in the bedroom. He can be missing the net 0 for 40 on the basketball court, but with you he scores every time.

If this has not been the case and you haven't established a win for him in the bedroom, you may have dribbled on your problem.

The good news is you can fix this by being creative and affirming. Get him to shoot and score.

If scoring is not happening at all, then it's time to have a conversation with your husband. Be understanding and compassionate. Perhaps you have no idea how to start a conversation or what to say. First, you wait for a good time and a good place. Timing is key. Second, approach him with humility and respect. Say something like this: "Sweetheart, I love you. I love to be close to you. Our physical relationship is very important to me, and I'd like to talk about what we can do to enhance our sex life. Maybe I'm doing something that is hurting our time together. What can I do—what can we do? Can we work on this together?"

Even Tougher Questions

It takes a brave woman to have considered the questions so far, and now to continue. Allow me to commend you for toughing it out and working toward solutions. Shall we keep going?

Has your husband felt manipulated, controlled, or bossed by you? Men can and will shut down sexually as a means of regaining control. If he is feeling manipulated or as if he is being stripped of his manhood, he may be withholding sex to get back at you. Yes, using sex as a weapon is unfair and you want to shout, "Penalty!" But let's be honest—who wants to have sex with someone who's bossy, controlling, or manipulative? I've spoken with many men who have confirmed this; they really do withhold intimacy as a way of regaining self-worth.

Before you dismiss this notion, I want to ask you a few more questions: Do you *tell* him to stop by the store on his way home, and not *ask* him? Do you order him to "take over the watch of the kids" when he comes through the door? Are you planning his schedule and then letting him know where he needs to be? Do you sometimes get mad at him for noncompliance? Do you give him the silent treatment when he does something you dis-agree with?

Is he allowed to say no to you? *No* is a powerful word, and one we all need to be able to use in our *healthy* relationships. If a person feels like they can't say no, they feel trapped and controlled. Can he say no without you giving him grief over it?

WHAT HE WANTS YOU TO KNOW:

"I felt so frustrated and emasculated. I was angry with you and decided I would withhold sex to gain control. I know it wasn't right, but it was a last resort."

—Paul, angry husband

"I wish you knew that the real me is just as scared, confused, and vulnerable as you are."

—John, trigger-shy husband

If your husband is feeling manipulated, controlled, or emasculated, these feelings very well could be your underlying problem. Be brave and ask him. It would go something like this: "Honey, I need to ask you something. Please be completely honest with me. I promise I won't overreact and I can handle the truth. Have I been bossy, controlling, or manipulative?"

Understand, some men may say no just to avoid the conflict they anticipate could arise if they were completely honest Assure him you really want to hear the truth.

Listen to his answer without saying a word. Encourage him to continue talking while you listen. When he is finished, ask for forgiveness. Assure him you will be working on your attitude and ask him to let you know as soon as you slip up.

If your treatment of your husband is the culprit, and he was indeed feeling slightly or significantly squashed, as soon as he sees you working on it *and* changing, your problems with a non-responsive husband will be over. O-v-e-r. His engine will rev up and this hiccup in your relationship will be only a distant memory. As long as you continue to keep yourself in check. Never emasculate your man.

WHAT HE WANTS YOU TO KNOW:

"I need validation as a man."

—Alex, newly married husband

"I need to be needed and valued. I want to be your rock."

—Darnell, married for twenty-five years

The Toughest Questions

One day my husband and I were sitting in a coffeehouse, and while my attention should have been on him, I allowed myself to become distracted. A well-dressed couple walked in who looked to be in their late forties. They were obviously married. As they walked through the door with her leading the way, she turned around and put out her open hand. "Give me the money," she said.

He handed her his wallet. I was totally hooked and intensely eavesdropping now.

Then she pointed and said, "You go sit over there." I was trying to be incognito but was totally staring.

Her tone was like that of a mother talking to a child, only this was her husband. After getting their drinks, she sat next to him, pulled out his wallet from *her bra*, and said, "So tell me, how was your day?"

Gulp! Did that just happen?

And this leads me to perhaps the most difficult set of questions yet.

You may have inadvertently adopted a mommy role instead of that of lover, wife, and honey, and therefore, this next section may require you to get gut-wrenchingly honest. Dear one, with more rockin' and rollin' as your goal, take a deep breath, and let's get hopping.

A man will not act like a chivalrous lover if he feels like he is wooing his mother. As his wife, you must be strategically careful not to function like a mom.

He wants to be the stud who gets the girl. He wants to passionately rescue his princess. He wants to be the gallant warrior who saves the kingdom. He wants to be your hero swooping in and saving the day.

Listen to what Dr. Kevin Leman says:

> Here's what you have to understand about that man of yours: He wants to be your hero. He wants to please you. And if you give him just the tiniest bit of encouragement, he'll go to the ends of the earth for you. But if you shoot him down, you might as well stick a dagger in his heart. He's going to slink away like a dog that's been beaten too many times and will just whimper by himself in his kennel. If you reluctantly accommodate his sexual needs, you will create a resentful husband who will seek pleasure, conversation, and intimacy elsewhere.[4]

Getting to the Nitty-Gritty

Do you find yourself giving commands such as, "You need to. . ." or "You should. . ." or asking, "Why did you. . ."? But you're just giving suggestions, right? No. That's mom-talk. Instead, *ask* if he'd like your thoughts, and refrain from questioning his every move. Always remember to approach him with respect. Many times the best thing we can do is be silent. I know this one really well because I can slip here quite easily. My husband will say sarcastically, "I'm glad you know what I should do; thank you for telling me." Oops, I did it again. At this point, I know to check myself and put Mommy away.

Do you get mad at him or just plain irked when he doesn't do what *you* want him to? He has a right as a grown man to do whatever he wants without "Mommy" trying to control him. Here's a hint, ladies: the more you give him room to do what he wants, the more he'll want to please you.

Do you ignore him as a means to make a point? Anyone who had a mother who gave them the "silent treatment" knows how terribly awful it is. It is not nice and usually is used to gain control. Shutting down when things don't go the way you want or when he doesn't meet your expectations is foul play.

Do you tell him, "I told you so"? Does anyone ever like to hear those words? That's what Mom says when she is utterly frustrated that you didn't take her advice. It's so easy to say, "I told you so," after things play out and all the facts are in. There have been plenty of times when I've been right about things, and there have been even more times when I've been totally wrong about things. Sometimes we are right and sometimes we are wrong, and shouting, "I told you so," only damages the relationship and causes your husband to feel worse than he already does. If he made a mistake, he knows it, and saying something about it will hurt him. Instead, offer sympathy and understanding, which just might get you closer to "jiving."

Do you yell at him or scold him? First, apologize and ask forgiveness, and then stop. No man deserves to be yelled at. You may be thinking, *Everyone yells from time to time, don't they?* Our speech can be used in a negative or positive way. Our tongues can shoot missiles. We can spew hurtful words and withhold adoration and praise.

Yelling is a sign of a deeper problem, and if you can't seem to stop, then getting help might be in order. Yelling and scolding is what moms do when they're losing control of their children. If you are yelling at him or scolding him, you are taking on a mothering role. Would you want to "take a roll" after being squawked at?

Are we having fun yet?

Do you ever belittle him? He may be laughing when you make a joke at his expense, but don't let the laugh fool you. Inside he may feel like retreating.

Have you ever talked *for* him? We've all known a woman who does this. Her husband will open his mouth to speak, and then she cuts him off and says it for him. Don't be *that woman*. And along the same line, don't correct him. Who cares if it was twelve donuts and not ten? It doesn't matter. On the other hand, being corrected *will* matter to him; he'll feel like a little boy, and you want a tiger.

Do you take care of things because he didn't do it on your timetable? It's like when you tell your kids to clean their rooms, then go and do it for them. That's what moms do. Maybe your husband takes on a project that he'll get done in *his* time, but you take it over because that's not fast enough for you. At the end of the day, if he drops something he said he'd take care of, then let him deal with the consequences. When he says he'll do something, trust him to do it. If you want to offer your help, or if both of you decide *together* that you'll work on said project *together*, that is completely different than doing it for him.

When he is driving—yes, I'm going there!—and needs to find a parking spot, do you tell him where to park? This is like when your teenager was learning to drive and you were continually giving instructions: "Slow down, careful on the turn. . . Pull in here. . . . Park in this spot." Chances are your man is completely capable of finding his own parking spot and has done so countless times without you. Imagine that!

Do you secretly think you know better than him? This is the way a mom thinks. It may be perfectly fine to have this mind-set with your children, but it is *not* fine with your spouse. If inside you are thinking you are usually right and he doesn't know as much as you, this attitude is going to pollute your relationship and could be the cause of less "bouncy-bouncy."

Have you expressed displeasure with your husband or been hypercritical of him? If a man feels like his wife is continually displeased with him, he will withdraw from closeness with her. Criticism causes resentment to fester and ultimately leads to a nonresponsive mate.

Recognizing an area that needs to change is the first and most painful step. Take a self-inventory and ask yourself if you've started acting like his mother—it takes a big woman to even admit this. And if indeed you have, it's never too late to turn it around. I'm sending you "spirit fingers" through these pages and cheering you on. Are you ready to turn your bedroom into a lovers' paradise filled with desire, appetite, and yearning?

Cue the sexy-time playlist.

It's time to start treating your husband like the fantasy man you want, and to keep treating him that way until he becomes the Casanova you desire. Focus on being his lover. Make him a priority in your home. Maybe you are a mom; if so, take time to remind him that you are his lover first. You can be a good mom to your kids *and* light the fire in your bedroom. Fill him up with manly stuff—respect, praise, appreciation, cheers, kisses, caresses, flashes (see chapter 8), and feminine attention.

Think back to when you were dating. What steps did you take to get ready when you knew you'd be seeing him? Give him the effort and attention you did while you were dating. In reality, you can treat him better than when you were dating because now you have more time together and more knowledge of what pleases him.

Do you want to be adored, brought flowers, given lots of attention?

Pursue him like a girlfriend hoping for a ring. Keep yourself from falling into a mommy role by asking yourself, "Would I do this if I were his girlfriend?"—only of course now you're his wife trying to woo him and not his girlfriend trying to win him.

Ask: If I were his girlfriend, would I neglect to thank him for opening the door for me? Would I constantly complain about petty things in my life? Would I get mad at him for forgetting to pick up his dry cleaning? Would I stop dressing up for him? Would I nag him like a squawking bird outside the window in the early morning hours? A girlfriend doesn't do those things. At least not one who is hoping to get a ring on her finger. She looks for ways to please her lady-killer. She looks for ways to build up. To praise. To cheer.

She doesn't tell him what to do. She offers to help.

Decide today that your husband is your champion, your conqueror, your superman, and put words to action.

Suggestions to fill his love tank:

- Say, *"I need your advice."* Look for ways to allow him to speak into your life.
- Ask, *"Can you help me, please?"* When he helps you and you are satisfied with his help, he feels valued.
- Proclaim, *"No one does this better than you."* When you look for his strengths and praise him for each one, you'll put a smirk on his face.

- *Accept "no" as an answer.* Respecting a person's "no" gives them value.
- *Say, "I can't do this as good as you."* I'm not suggesting you lie here. Consider your weaknesses that perhaps are his strengths.
- *Say, "Thank you!"* Do it as often as possible each day. Thank him for things he does, and thank him for things he doesn't do. Your Don Juan loves to hear "Thank you."
- *Ask, "Will you open this jar, please?"* This reminds him of how strong he is.
- *Proclaim, "You bailed me out when [insert noble act]."* This reminds him of how smart he is.
- *Assert, "You rescued me when you [insert chivalrous act]."* This reminds him that you want him.
- *Say, "Your opinion matters to me—please share it with me."* This tells him you value his input and gives him a feeling of accomplishment.
- *Tell him, "Your recommendation worked."* When he's right, announce it.
- *Say, "Sex with you in the morning starts my day off right."* This lets him know how much you appreciate him.
- *Declare, "All I want to do is fall into your arms at the end of the day."* Saying something like this communicates your desire for him.
- *Ask, "Will you hold me?"* Ask for what you want; don't assume he knows.
- *Tell him, "You feel strong and smell great."* What man wouldn't want to hear that?
- *Say, "I trust you."* This tells him you're his biggest fan.
- *Tell him, "You made a great decision when [insert valiant deed]."* This says you trust and value him.
- *Say, "I am so proud of you."* This one statement conveys heaps of praise to him.

- *Tell him, "I like it when you [fill in the action]."* This affirms him.
- *Lavish him with kisses.* Kissing sends a message to him and to your body.
- *Wake him early with caresses.* This could lead to driving Miss Daisy.
- *Plan dates.* Date nights are essential to a spicy marriage and are a time when you can remind him of why he married you.
- *Touch him often.* Hold his hand, sit close, graze him when you pass, rub his shoulders, massage his feet, touch, touch, touch.

When your husband's love tank is jam-packed, it's highly probable his affection will pour out. The goal is to remind him that he's a hunky man, and then his hunkiness will spill out—and pour on you.

With any progress you do make, enjoy your time together. Even if your engagements are not as frequent as you'd like, be thankful and appreciate each encounter. Keep pursuing him.

Most likely this is not exactly what you want—you want him to pursue you with an insatiable passion and desire. Be realistic: ramping things up is probably going to take some time. Every little bit of progress you make brings you that much closer to the Romeo you long for. Take what you can get and be happy with it. Have a good attitude and don't give up. Do what you need to do to get the electric marriage you crave.

SECRET SEX MISSION #9

This is your mission if you wish to accept it: Are you ready to take on one of the hardest challenges yet? This mission is to ask him, "What can I do to help you today?" for thirty days in a row.

Focus on serving him. Be a servant and have an attitude of humility. Above all, do not expect *anything* in return. Take thirty days to love him unconditionally with words and with actions. (If you are thinking this has nothing to do with sex, you are completely wrong. How we treat our spouses affects our overall relationships, including our sex lives.)

ASK HIM

Find out ways he feels loved by you. Ask him what words, activities, and gestures best communicate that you love him. Ask him what you do that causes him to feel loved.

PART 4

BRINGING IT ALL TOGETHER

CHAPTER 10

KEEP THE ENGINE RUNNING

> NOT TONIGHT, HONEY—
> THE DOG DRANK MY COFFEE.

We were on a road trip, and Jeff and I decided to pull over to the side of the road and have sex." It's not often you hear something like that from one of your friends. Adrienne continued, "We were towing our boat and it was the middle of the night, and we thought why not? So we pulled over and hid behind the boat. Then when we got home and were unpacking. Jeff was in the garage. He's task-oriented, so he was focused on getting everything put away. Being tired and a little grumpy, Jeff started barking orders at me. I was getting offended. Right about that time, Lauren, who was housesitting for us, walked up from across the street, but I didn't see her." (Lauren is their daughter Amanda's twenty-one-year-old friend.) Adrienne continued, "As I backed up the car to do an errand, I stuck my head out of the car window and yelled at him, 'What happened to the guy that I just had sex with on the side of the road?!' Then Jeff looked up and said, 'Hi, Lauren.' She just stood there staring at us. It was pretty funny. But then, later, we told Amanda the story because we felt since her friend knew that we had sex on the side of the road, she should probably know that also. And you should have seen her face!" Adrienne laughed, saying, "At least she knows her parents still have a good marriage."

Who says waka-waka gets boring over time?

That's what we will be exploring in this chapter: how we can keep the love flowing. I'll also be lifting the veil on my own marriage of nearly four decades a bit more. Are you ready to have some fun?

It All Starts with You

In 1935 a new product hit the scene that empowered women all over the globe. It was called Jean Naté. As a young child, I can remember my mother lavishly applying this after-bath splash all over herself as droplets flew throughout the bathroom. The smell of citrus and jasmine—the fresh scent of sunshine filling the air. This was the scent of a take-charge woman. I thought if you were married you had to douse yourself with Jean Naté, and the commercials confirmed it. If you wanted to be a powerful, sexy woman, this fragrance turned you into a minx who could conquer any man.

As I got older, a commercial for Enjoli perfume, to the tune of "I'm a Woman," told women that frying bacon, flashing cash, dancing, and spraying perfume on yourself turned you into a sex kitten. These things were what gave women their power and their sex appeal. The message was that a woman can cook, work, look like a model, and still lavish her man with love at the end of the day. Hitting the US pop charts in 1963, "I'm a Woman" sung by Peggy Lee said it all.

Could these advertisements be on to something? How we see ourselves and what we think and project about our sexuality will have huge effects on our love lives.

What causes you to feel sensual? What brings a spring to your sexy? What draws out your feminine mystic? Is it dancing around with a frying pan or dousing yourself in a fragrance or just simply shaving your legs? What is it? Do you know?

When we love someone deeply, selflessly, we feel compelled to be the best version of ourselves possible so we can bring that into the relationship. We work on being the best we can be. When we sharpen *us*, we sharpen our marriages. Marriage draws out the real us, both the beautiful and the ugly, leaving us bare and prompting us to reflect on the persons we are becoming. Working on our marriages means working on ourselves.

Dr. Gary Smalley tells us in *The DNA of Relationships*, "Taking good care of yourself is actually a godly thing. It's always in the best interest of all parties involved. Why? Because only when you're full do you have the resources to care for others. You cannot fully extend yourself unless you operate from fullness. And you never will get full unless you take good care of yourself."[1]

When we nurture ourselves and pamper our bodies so that we look and feel good, this extra care lights up a flashing sign saying Open for Business. When we don't feel good about ourselves, we will be tempted to keep the Closed sign up. Does your sign say Closed or Open?

As women we are pulled in multiple directions at once, yet because we only have so much energy, we need to prioritize what matters most to us. Kids, career, church, friends, hobbies—all are significant and noble aspirations. Does feeling desirable and sexy even make your priority list? Stop for a minute and give yourself a score from 1 to 10, with 10 being the highest, for where you see yourself on the sensual scale. If you can give yourself a 7 or higher, that comes with a pat on the back and a victory dance. But if your rating is disappointing, don't despair. You can change that.

WHAT HE WANTS YOU TO KNOW:

"I want you to spend some time on yourself; please take time for you."

—Charles, concerned husband

Randomly my husband will look at me like he's about to make a wise or profound observation, then remark, "Thank you for taking care of yourself."

"Um, you're welcome?"

Then I wait. Was that a pick-up line? Nope. He was only sincerely expressing his appreciation.

When you prioritize pampering yourself and feeling "sassy," you prioritize your husband. The more you nurture yourself, the more energy you'll bring to your relationship. It's not about looking like a model or getting plastic surgery; it's about making the effort to look good. Men notice the effort and appreciate it. Oddly enough, your attention to yourself makes your husband feel loved.

Five Simple Reminders about Lasting Love

The first step in keeping the engine running is to have the engine turned on, and that starts with you as you take charge of your sexuality. In other words, pay attention to what gets your engine going, and also pay attention to what stalls you out. Keep the following factors in mind to help enrich your love life.

1. Smells Are Important

This one may seem like a no-brainer, but you'd be surprised how many women don't consider the smell factor. Make sure the aromas of all his personal care products lure you in and don't propel you away. Scent plays a huge role in how close we want to get to our spouses. I'm willing to bet he will gladly toss anything that is a deterrent.

2. Keeping Things Fresh and Fun Is Key

When we get into our day-to-day routines, we may forget to take time to have fun with each other. Scheduling fun may seem odd, but it's necessary. If you and your man aren't spending many enjoyable moments together, it's time to make fun happen. But how? Ask him to tell you some fun things he likes to do, and tell him what you consider fun. Having fun together leads to more horizontal hokeypokey—because you'll want to—which leads to a stronger marriage. Couples who play together stay together.

In her book *For Women Only*, Shaunti Feldhahn writes that one man she surveyed said, "All the other men are definitely jealous when they see another man out with his wife on the golf course—without a doubt."[2]

3. Date Nights Strengthen Your Relationship

I'm friends with a couple who have a regular—set in cement—practice of going on a date every Monday night. In fact, they call it Mon-date. She will tell you that bringing out all of her feminine charm and being as girly as possible is something she looks forward to every week. He says this Mon-date is just as important as going to church, and for him that's a high priority because he's a pastor. All seven of their kids will tell you not to mess with Mom and Dad on Mon-date night. Dating your spouse and reminding each other why you got married in the first place will spice up any marriage. If you aren't going on dates with your honey, you can change that today.

4. Can We Talk about Kissing?

"Ewwww!" screeched our toddler grandson as my husband and I kissed.

WHAT HE WANTS YOU TO KNOW:

"Why are you complaining about our sex life and saying it's not frequent enough? You won't even kiss me. Why would I try to go any further?"
—Damien, divorced husband

Kissing communicates a lot. I'm guessing that kissing was a big part of your courtship. How often do you kiss during the day? Kissing is like lowering the drawbridge for passion. It keeps you thinking about each other all day. It's quick. It's easy. It's fun. Unfortunately, many married couples stop kissing shortly after settling into marriage. You don't have to be one of those couples. Let others say, "Ewwww!"

5. Sex Is Fun and Enhances Marriage

While I was chatting with a group of ladies about marriage, one blurted out, "Oh, you'll never believe what I had to do to get my new kitchen!" None of us asked what it was, but she made it pretty clear it was sexual, and far out of the realm of what was usual for them. This makes for a good story but not a good marriage. (Incidentally, this couple later got divorced.)

If you are bargaining with your husband over sex, you are hurting your relationship. The bedroom is not a place for selfish parleys. He's not buying a used car, right? When we start negotiating inside and outside of the bedroom—to get under the sheets—our relationship suffers. It would be like him saying, "Honey, if you do the laundry, then I'll talk to you tonight." Totally not cool. This kind of bargaining puts a block on love. Just remember how amazing sex is: you get to be held, caressed, and loved in a way no one else can love you. Keep the love flowing mentally and physically.

One time a young lady asked to meet with me. She had been married for roughly two difficult years.

"He's really mean," she said, "and I can't take it anymore."

We talked for a while, and then I asked her how her sex life was going. "Oh, I cut him off," she proclaimed. "That's all I have to get back at him with."

I said, "Sweetheart, if someone put you in a cage and didn't give you any food or water, would you be nice to them? That is in essence what you are doing to him. I'm sure he's feeling very frustrated and doesn't know what to do." This young bride became pregnant a few months later. Hmm.

If sex is not part of your regular routine, ask yourself why. When a marriage is void of passion, both parties are left vulnerable.

In *Have a New Husband by Friday*, Dr. Kevin Leman writes, "A happy, satisfied husband will do anything for you, including going to Bed, Bath & Beyond to help you lug that $500 comforter set back home. He might even help you set it up."[3]

We can make choices that turn off our engines, or we can make choices that turn on our engines. Cutting him off does not give him an excuse to have an affair, but it does leave him, *and yourself*, vulnerable to one. Don't send him out into the world vulnerable. When you make sexual rendezvous a regular habit, you will find that the more you have sex, the more you'll want sex—because we were created with the desire for connection.

Jesus said, "Have you not read that He who created them from the beginning MADE THEM MALE AND FEMALE, and said, 'FOR THIS REASON A MAN SHALL LEAVE HIS FATHER AND MOTHER AND BE JOINED TO HIS WIFE, AND THE TWO SHALL BECOME ONE FLESH'? So they are no longer two, but one flesh. What therefore God has joined together, let no man separate" (Matthew 19:4–6).

Keep Improving Your Marriage

It was Christmas morning, the time our family traditionally opens our Christmas gifts to each other. As I unwrapped a somewhat unusual gift from my husband, it became clear why he gave it to me before the kids were up. It was a book about sex. *Really?* Not exactly a gift one expected from Santa. I was feeling a bit confused and wondered if he was trying to send me a message. I had thought we were doing fine—actually, better than fine—but maybe I was wrong.

Then Mike said, "Uh, this gift comes with an explanation." I was all ears. *Okay, lay it on me.*

"Um, Pastor Tim recommended this book to us pastors and encouraged us to give a copy to our wives. So I thought I'd make it one of your Christmas gifts." Well then, if Pastor Tim recommended it, that was good enough for me, and I read every page of the book.

It was a book about how one couple amplified their love life through a commitment to engage in sex regularly—actually 101 days in a row. Now, that's a serious commitment! They called it their "sex experiment." The biggest takeaway for me was how it improved their marriage—in every way. Their communication got better. They worked together better as a team. The fun in their relationship increased. They held hands more. Time spent together went from making quick Target runs to hanging out in hip coffee shops. They bonded in a way they hadn't in the past. And their conflicts became easier to resolve.

Say what? These are definitely points to stop and ponder. Wouldn't you agree?

Imagine

What would happen if both you and your husband knew—absolutely knew—you'd have sex often? No matter what—no matter what, what, what—it would be a priority in your life. What if this was a commitment to each other, for better or for worse? What do you think would happen? How would your relationship change?

I was thinking about this very thing today. My husband and I had a conflict. Imagine what it would be like to be writing a book like this and be out of sync with your true love. My husband and I are both passionate people, and sometimes our passions collide. If you're married, I'm sure you understand. In writing this section, I realized something I had never considered over the course of our decades together. Think about the last time you had a disagreement with your husband. Aren't disagreements usually about someone's feelings getting hurt?

At the core of most marital conflicts is a hurt: one or both accidentally hurt the other, and one or both lash out. This is what was happening between me and my husband, and it was the reason we were out of sync. When these types of you-hurt-my-feelings-so-I-will-put-up-my-guard spats happen, and there seems to be a wedge between us, there is something my husband and I both do. I noticed it for the first time today. We do really nice things for each other. As in, I'm angry with you, and I'm letting you know I'm angry, but I'm still going to be nice to you. I cooked him breakfast while he slept. He made our bed. I kissed him on the cheek. He called me beautiful. He was going to head to the grocery store so I could write. All this while we were both totally irked and hurt because of the other. We ended up having breakfast on our front porch and talking through our issue. Then we headed to the store together, in sync once again. Even when we don't "feel" crazy in love, we "act" in love, which allows us to work through our struggles more quickly.

Nobody wants to get naked with someone they're angry with. Sex on a regular basis forces you to get along.

There's a colossal difference between falling in love and staying in love. Falling in love comes naturally. It's easy; it's euphoric. Staying in love takes strategic planning. It takes intentionality; it takes work. How do we continue wanting what we already have? We have to create desire. Create wanting. Create anticipation of the unknown. We must create the fantasy of the everyday. We have to wow! the ho-hum. We must do things differently and keep changing what used to be different. We have to keep inserting surprises in our normal lives.

Surprises

When our older two children were beginning to talk and walk, my husband and I would send "love notes" to each other via our children. As they got older and could run faster, our game became even more fun. It went something like this: Go tell Mommy she's hot. Go tell Daddy that Mommy has a surprise for him. With fun coded love messages, the kids would run from one end of the house to the other, which always made them laugh, wore them out, and filled the house with excitement. It created an element of surprise in the ordinary of our day-to-day.

Until. . .yeah, you guessed it, they began to figure out the "fun coded messages" and our fun game was over. But while it lasted it was one of our favorite family activities and more fun than any board game.

Another game we played when our kids were young was the roll-the-ball-and-name-an-animal game. Our family would get into a circle on the floor and roll a ball to one another. When the ball came to one of us, we had to name an animal. Dog, cat, gorilla. Whatever animal came to mind.

One time my husband said, "Mommy in bed."

The kids laughed at the thought of Mom being an animal but were too young to consider any other alternative. I gave him *the look* and didn't give it another thought. That is, until I was picking up the babysitter, a homeschooled teenage girl from our church. My daughter proudly announced, "My daddy says that my mommy is an animal in bed."

I. Was. Mortified.

Frankly, I didn't know what to say, so I didn't say anything to our sweet, innocent, and soon-to-be-overpaid babysitter.

While we're on the topic of overpaid babysitters, one time I hired a babysitter for the day and got a day rate for a hotel room. If you're wondering, yes, it was uber awkward checking into the hotel that day, but I pushed through because I was on a mission to let my husband know how valuable he was to me. After making sure my husband's calendar was cleared for the afternoon, I invited him out for lunch. During our meal, I gave him a card with the hotel key inside. I wish there was a way I could show you the look on his face when he opened it. Think expressions of people who've just won the lottery. It was totally worth all the awkwardness I had to work through.

Another time my husband came home to a dark and empty house. I left a note on the kitchen table sealed with a lipstick kiss. It read, "Meet me at [name of restaurant]." The lipstick kiss told him what kind of night I had in mind.

Here's one on the cheap. I call it Hot Dog Night. When our kids were young, I'd prepare hot dogs for them (a treat they didn't get often) and fun foods they liked to eat. After their early dinner, the kids got to watch a movie in a dark room. They thought it was later than it actually was, and they were in bed before you could say, "Dad's home!" I prepared a romantic dinner for my husband—candlelight, rose petals, soft music—and I dressed up like we were going out on the town. Everyone was happy. Every time I informed the kids it was Hot Dog Night, they were almost as happy as their dad was when I told him. You don't need to have kids to celebrate Hot Dog Night; it's a great date on the cheap.

These were all big hits, but I want to share a huge fail too, just for fun. I was home alone and my husband was working late. I decided I wanted to cheer him up after what was probably a long, tough day for him. My plan was to open the door for him naked. I felt hungry and made myself some dinner and sat on the sofa, eating and waiting. I felt cold, so I grabbed a blanket. Next thing

I knew the door swung open and in walked our teenage son, who wasn't supposed to be home until much later. Thank goodness I had been cold! He said, "Are you naked? Why are you eating dinner naked?" I said, "No questions, just go to your room." Minutes later my husband got home. Yes, seeing me in the nude did put a skip in his step. *Surprise!* But then I had to tell him our son had arrived home before him. Epic fail.

Lipstick messages on the bathroom mirror, notes placed for him to find, racy texts, surprise trysts, breakfast in bed—our expressions of love can be as grand as our imaginations.

Suggestions to light things up:

- When you have to clean up a spill, show off your assets.
- Let him know when you're changing and invite him to watch.
- Dance for him and with him.
- Leave your lacy underwear in his suit pocket.
- Pass him a love note during dinner with a promise of "dessert."
- Wake him up in the middle of the night with a little "surprise."
- Buy new underclothing.
- Be eager and responsive.
- Buy a new negligee or sexier pajamas.
- Plan a date for monster mash.

He'll be all over it. And you.

Keep the Love Flowing

Maybe you're concerned that things have stalled out in your love life. You want to improve the pulse of your relationship but fear he may not be as interested as you are. Be honest with yourself.

When was the last time he asked you to join him in the shower? When was the last time he asked you to join him in a romantic liaison? When was the last time he asked for time alone with you? Is it possible that he has given up on trying to keep the engine running because he's so used to being turned down? It takes two to tango, but it only takes one to change things up.

Could it be he's more sensitive emotionally than you thought?

Men protect themselves from emotional pain, Shaunti Feldhahn explains in *The Male Factor*. They may have a tough exterior persona, which serves to protect their vulnerable interior self, but it's just a facade. Most women don't realize how sensitive men really are.[4]

If we want to keep things electric and flowing, we have to create a safe environment where love can flourish and thrive. Flood him with lavish praise for who he is as a man, and let words of affirmation and adoration pour from your mouth. Building up our men with words of praise reinforces our love connections and amplifies romance. What we think, and then what we say will have a profound effect on our hearts. Tell him he's sexy. And desirable. And wanted.

Build him up not only with your words, but with your actions too. Go to his sports events, sit with him while he works outside, hang out with him while he is in his home office, and be interested in what he is interested in. Be willing to play with him inside *and* outside of the bedroom.

We all know things in motion tend to stay in motion. Once our love boats start picking up momentum, each sexual encounter leads to the next. Especially when we fully trust our partners. Trust is built by how we treat each other throughout the day. Honor goes back and forth. As we stay connected through gentle touches, entwined hands, passionate kisses, and tender caresses, the intimacy we share never ends. It just keeps getting better and better.

And an occasional lap dance doesn't hurt either. Joke? Okay. . .not kidding. When we keep things moving, sexual energy flows naturally out of the love and respect we display back and forth all day.

Throughout the writing of this chapter, I've been listening to a certain song over and over and replaying it in my head. It's a song performed by the artist Cher titled "If I Could Turn Back Time," written by Diane Warren. Originally, when the song was introduced to Cher, she didn't want to record it. Warren begged her, and reports say she grabbed Cher's leg and said, "You've got to record it!" Cher's response was not very favorable. She told Warren, "You're hurting my leg!" but she agreed to give the song a try. "If I Could Turn Back Time" was released in 1989 and was a huge hit.

The song's piercing lyrics are about a love that is lost due to carelessness. If only I could turn back time and take back my hurtful words and careless actions. If only I wasn't too proud to admit when I was wrong and ask for forgiveness. If only I knew why I did the things I did, because I didn't mean to hurt you. All I want is for you to love me again. If I had another chance I'd give you my all, if only I could turn back time. The song reminds us that words can be used like weapons to wound another. "If I Could Turn Back Time" resonated with millions of people, perhaps because the lyrics were all too personal and true.

We can't turn back time, but we can change our futures. I urge you not to become complacent about your love life. Keep the eroticism alive in your marriage. Keep the energy flowing. Love your husband. Honor him. Praise him. Thank him. Kiss him. Touch him. That's the prescription for keeping the sexual momentum in motion.

SECRET SEX MISSION #10

This is your mission if you wish to accept it: Give your relationship a jump start by thinking of a creative way to change things up. Plan a surprise for him. But don't stop there. Keep brainstorming ways to keep your relationship fresh and fun. Give it a try and see if he's not lugging that comforter set around for you.

ASK HIM

What types of fun activities would your husband like to experience with you? Ask him for ways you can have fun together as a couple.

CHAPTER 11

SEX, PANCAKES, AND WHAT WOMEN WANT

> NOT TONIGHT, HONEY—
> I BOUGHT A BAG OF CHOCOLATE KISSES,
> AND I PLAN ON EATING THE WHOLE BAG.

Story 1

She wondered if she should say anything. Would he think she was strange? A little goofy, maybe?

What if he laughs at me? It might be best to keep this to myself, Becky thought.

But one day she blurted it out. "I have a fantasy."

Well, that got Ted's attention. After twenty years of marriage, getting Ted's attention wasn't the easiest task.

With Ted's undivided focus on her, she said, "I want to have sex and then make pancakes together."

Ted blinked twice in surprise. After taking a moment to think, he nodded and said, "Okay. We can do that."

And then she waited, eagerly anticipating the day he would finally act on her request. A week went by. Then a month. Then six months. And still no action.

Maybe I shouldn't have said anything at all, Becky thought. She decided to broach the subject again when they were alone—but that was rare with two kids, one in middle school and one in high school.

"Ted, do you remember that fantasy I told you about?"

His attention was recaptured. "What fantasy?"

"The one about sex and pancakes," Becky said, feeling a bit weird.

"Oh, that. Were you serious about that?"

"Yes," she replied, even though she was tempted to say no.

"Okay," Ted said once again. "We can do that."

And she waited. . .

And again nothing. . .

And then. . .

One day when Becky picked up Sarah from middle school, she got in the car clearly upset.

"I am so mad!" Sarah exclaimed. "I have Saturday school!"

Trying not to overreact, Becky asked, "For what?"

"For being late too many times," Sarah said with disgust. "This is so lame!"

Becky thought to herself, *Well, she was late, so this is good. This could mean less stress for me in the mornings if she learns her lesson and gets her act together. And I didn't have to say anything!*

Becky told her daughter, "Sorry, honey. What exactly does this mean?"

"I have to be at school at eight in the morning on a Saturday and sit in detention."

"Until when?"

"One in the afternoon!" Sarah slouched in her seat. "Going to be the worst day of my life!"

The rest of the drive passed in silence as Becky drove to pick up Jack from school. As she parked and waited for Jack to come to the car, not a word was spoken as Sarah stewed in the front seat.

Jack broke the silence as he swung the rear door open with shouts of, "Stupid! Stupid idiots!" Jack whined like a four-year-old as he got into the car and slammed the door.

"Thank you for slamming my door," Becky said as she and Sarah exchanged looks.

"The coach called an extra practice on Saturday because of those idiot freshmen!" Jack continued.

"At least you don't have detention!" Sarah shouted back at him.

"Stupid idiots!" Jack repeated. "I don't even know how they made the team!"

Becky wanted to laugh but held it in. "This Saturday?"

"Yes," Jack replied. "Stupid idiots!"

"What time?"

"Seven thirty in the morning," Jack said. "Can you believe it? Who gets up that early on a Saturday? I'm so mad!"

Becky's mind was calculating. *Okay, 7:30 and then 8:00. I'll have a Saturday morning alone with Ted!* She was the only happy one in the car.

The long-awaited day finally arrived. Becky woke up early and went for a run. She drove Jack to his practice and Sarah to detention, the pair of them miserable. But *she* was floating.

Would Ted be awake when she arrived back home? She decided that if he was still sleeping, she would let him sleep. He'd had a tough week at work and could use the extra rest. It began to rain on her way home. She listened to the sound of it hitting her car, a tranquil rhythm. This would be the perfect morning to finally act on her fantasy.

As Becky pulled into the driveway, the light rain had turned into a downpour. She hopped out of the car and landed in a big puddle. Her tennis shoes were soaked. As she came through the door, she was greeted not by her husband, but by the family bulldog Bullwinkle.

Ted must still be sleeping. *Sigh.* Becky decided to quietly open the bedroom door. She peeked in and saw Ted lying there, sound asleep. *Oh well. Another time*, she thought to herself as she slowly closed the door.

As she started to walk away, she felt the squishing of her cold, wet feet. She considered grabbing her cozy slippers. They were just inches past the door.

Carefully, she opened the bedroom door again. As she gently reached for the slippers, she could feel the full power and strength of Bullwinkle fly past her. He barreled into the room, running around and then jumping on the bed.

"Ted! I am so sorry!" Becky exclaimed.

"It's okay," Ted responded. "This was a fun way to be woken up."

Becky took a deep breath. "Sex and pancakes?" As the words left her lips, she already feared they would be rejected.

"Okay," Ted said without hesitation.

"Really?" Becky said casually in an attempt to hide her excitement.

"Yes," Ted replied. "What kind of pancakes?"

"Does it matter?"

"Blueberry?"

"Absolutely," Becky said, "but you have to help me cook them. Okay?"

"Okay," Ted said, confirming that he was on board with her request.

"Let me take a quick shower, and I'll join you," Becky said. Since she had gone for a run, she needed to pretty up.

"Sounds good," Ted responded. "I'm not going anywhere."

While Becky was in the shower, her mind was racing. She didn't want him to fall back asleep, but even in her hurry she made sure to shave her legs. She thought about Ted while she hurried.

Becky finished her shower, dried off, and slipped into some lingerie. The room was dark, and she could hear the sound of the rain hitting the roof. As she slid into bed next to her husband, she thought about how perfect it all was, and how glad she was the dog had woken him. She wasn't bashful in expressing her desire for him.

Ted took his time and took control.

Becky was glad she didn't wimp out on her seemingly silly request. She and Ted went into the kitchen for phase two, an equal element of the fantasy for her—an element she knew Ted couldn't really understand—and they prepared pancakes together. Becky lit a candle and placed it on the kitchen table. Their hands touched as they both reached for the measuring cup. She pulled him close and kissed him. "Thank you," Becky sighed. "This means a lot to me."

Sitting down for their late breakfast, Becky said, "Let's do this again."

"For sure," Ted said, smiling.

They talked as they ate their blueberry pancakes at the kitchen table, with Bullwinkle underneath, and a quiet house for just those few hours. It was worth the wait.

Story 2

Jackie dressed up for a night out. She had waited all week with anticipation for a reprieve from her daily responsibilities—work, meal preparation, dirty dishes, and the piles of laundry that never seemed to diminish. After showering, carefully applying makeup, spending extra time on her hair, and sliding into an elegant dress and heels, she glanced at herself in the full-length mirror and thought, *Dang, girl, you look good!* Feeling confident, sexy, and adventurous, she strutted out the door as she listened to the clicking of her heels.

She found a seat in the lounge of an upscale restaurant and ordered a mint soda and truffle fries. Jackie sat, sipped her drink, slowly savored her fries, and relaxed. *Grown-up time at last.*

She looked up and noticed him walk through the door of the restaurant. Butterflies fluttered in her stomach. *Whoa, he's hot.* She eyed him up and down and smiled. *Man, he's handsome, and so well dressed. I love a man in a suit.* When the hostess asked him if he'd like a table, he declined and headed for the lounge.

He sat near Jackie and ordered an Arnold Palmer. Then he looked at Jackie with a half grin. "Are you waiting for someone?"

"No," said Jackie as she turned her body toward him.

"I'm Ron, by the way," he said as he scooted closer. What's your name?"

"Jackie."

And so began their rally of questions. Ron learned of Jackie's four kids and her appreciation for art, and Jackie learned about Ron's business and love for the Dallas Cowboys. They talked and asked each other questions back and forth with complete attention on the other.

They'd talked for almost an hour when Ron asked, "Would you like to join me for dinner?" Jackie quickly agreed. Ron walked over to the hostess and asked for a table for two. As they sat down in a cozy oval-shaped booth, Ron slipped his hand into Jackie's. She could feel a tingle throughout her body.

Soon a server approached their table. "I'm sorry to disturb you"—they were so focused on each other that their server felt hesitant to interrupt them—"but can I tell you about our specials this evening?" They listened to the specials, but they were thinking only of each other.

Ron couldn't keep his eyes off her and would occasionally softly run his hand up her leg. Jackie could smell the enticing aroma of his cologne and frequently tapped her foot against his. Even before their food arrived, Ron slowly and gently kissed her. Their conversation throughout dinner was engaging, with both learning secrets about the other that one doesn't usually tell so easily and quickly. When the check came, Ron handed the server his credit card before she could even place the bill on the table. Jackie was thankful he eliminated any awkwardness over paying the bill. While Ron was signing the receipt, Jackie quickly glanced over and noticed he had left a huge tip. She thought to herself, *Generosity—such a great quality in a man.*

Ron gazed at her, and for the first time she could sense a bit of nervousness coming from him as he said, "I have a room at the Glenmere Hotel. Would you like to join me?" Jackie nodded her head yes. They left the restaurant and headed over to his hotel, holding hands as they walked. When Jackie entered his room, she noticed it wasn't just a room, but a beautiful suite. They spent the night together. In the morning, Jackie nuzzled up to Ron, and when he opened his eyes he said, "Good morning, beautiful. . . . I love you." "I love you," Jackie responded as she kissed him. Neither of them felt any guilt or remorse. Because they. . .were. . .married.

Story 3

It was a hot summer night. Lynette was tossing and turning, unable to sleep. The night was quiet. Until, as if the floodgates had opened, a downpour of rain began. She could hear the sound of the rain hitting the roof. Calming. Rhythmic. She loved the rain. Sam rolled over. She still found him handsome even after twenty-six years of marriage.

He opened his eyes. "Can't sleep?" he said softly as she turned toward him.

"Nope," Lynette said with frustration.

Sam grinned. "It's raining."

"I know," she responded.

Then he said something she'd been waiting to hear for such a long time she almost forgot she had shared it with him.

"How about I grab a blanket and we go outside in the backyard?"

"*Yes!*" she said with excitement.

Sam smiled.

Lynette said, "Make sure the kids are sleeping."

Sam laughed. "Okay."

Sam got up and grabbed a blanket from the closet. Lynette wrapped herself in another blanket while Sam checked on the kids.

"All clear," Sam said.

And they went into their backyard for some diddle-diddle in the dark, in the rain, under the stars, hidden behind the clouds, on top of the blanket Sam laid down. It was better than Lynette had imagined. Once they got back in the house and dried off, Lynette looked at Sam and said, "Thank you. I can't believe you remembered."

"Of course I did. I listen to you." He kissed her on the forehead. "Happy?"

"Very," she said with an inhale and a smirk.

What about You?

Do you have a fantasy? Or a few? Or many, maybe? Would it surprise you that most people do? Men and women alike have sexual fantasies. Have you ever felt ashamed for any erotic musings that have roamed through your head? Guess what? If your thoughts have ever taken a stroll a bit on the wild side. . .you're normal. We are sexual beings, and sexual thoughts come to sexual beings. Maybe you'd like to be adventurous and act on some of those thoughts. As long as you stay within God's design for marriage, and your partner is on board, why not go for it? What could it hurt? It might liven up your jingle-jangle time and your connection. When a marriage gets stronger, everyone involved wins.

The more wins we create in marriage, the stronger our foundations of love, trust, and longing become.

Maybe you feel like your whims and imaginings are silly and you would be embarrassed to share them with your husband. There's nothing silly about enhancing your marriage and building a stronger foundation. If it can bring a little excitement to the blasé of your routine, why not explore and be adventurous? It doesn't have to be grandiose. It can be something very simple, like walking hand in hand along the beach and then going home to be alone. Or perhaps it's something a bit racier. Whatever gets *you* racing—that's all that matters. Most men would happily comply if only you would communicate your desires.

Sexual fun can't always be about him; it has to be about you too. His reaching climax is pretty much a sure thing; any loving husband would be happy to make getting busy a *boom!* for both of you.

What do *you* want?

What do *you* desire?

Many women like the feeling of surrendering control. They want the feeling of someone else taking care of them. . .want to feel desired and wanted. . .want to escape from reality. Do you know what you want? What enables you to receive pleasure fully?

Communication is the key. I think we all can agree that our husbands' thought processes and communication styles are very different from our own. You need to communicate in a way that clearly defines what you want and how important it is for you. Sometimes it means being persistent.

In Story 1, Becky's sex and pancakes fantasy, she easily could have given up, thinking she had clearly communicated her desires *already*. In her own mind, she could have been justified resolving herself to feelings of rejection and anger. But giving up on her fantasy would not have been a good choice. It wouldn't have been good for her or for her marriage. Reading over that story, you probably thought Becky *did* communicate clearly, over and over, and that she had a right to feel rejected and angry. But it wasn't until the house was empty and the stars aligned that she was able to *clearly* communicate in a way Ted understood. And not only that, but Ted had the opportunity to respond, and he happily did so.

Be persistent in striving to make your marriage the best it can be. Practice good communication skills in the "accommodation" department. It won't just rev up your boom-boom time; it will deepen your bond and enrich your entire relationship.

Desire

My two-year-old grandson—yes, I'm telling a story about my grandbaby—was playing outside with my daughter and son-in-law.

He started yelling, "Car! Car!"

His mom asked, "Do you want to go for a car ride?"

"Yes!"

Figuring they all could use a change of scenery, they got in the car, and when the little guy was snug in his car seat, my daughter asked, "Where do you want to go?"

He said, "Tartit [Target]."

And they all went to Target. He knew exactly what he wanted and asked for it.

Oftentimes, as women, we are the ones taking care of everyone around us, and we will forfeit our own needs and desires. This mentality can trickle into the bedroom too. Have you given up on asking for what you want? When did it become not okay to ask for what you desire?

Ladies, do you want to get your husband's undivided attention? Tell him you want to talk about sex. His ears will perk up, and he may even remove any distractions. Couples talk about all sorts of household and relational topics—schedules, the kids, grocery shopping, who hurt whose feelings, the laundry—yet sex rarely makes the top twenty if it gets on the list at all.

In a loving relationship both parties can talk about their fantasies and wants without ridicule or judgment. The key is to give your husband an environment where he can talk about his struggles and desires without fear of shame, embarrassment, or repercussions. You just might find that many of your desires line up, but if they don't, try not to dismiss his thoughts. Give yourself time to mull them over for a while. You may come up with an alternative you both will enjoy.

When talking about your own desires, focus in on what you like as opposed to what you don't like. Remember, even if your husband has a tough exterior, he can be very sensitive, especially about pleasing you. Caution and carefully chosen words are in order. Emphasizing what you like will take you further than keying in on anything negative. If, however, you have any "issues" you need to discuss, be extra gentle and kind. Also, be aware that there are ways of "telling" him what you like without using actual words.

I recall hearing about a classroom experiment. The room was full of students who seemed tired, uninterested, and bored with what the teacher was saying, except for when the teacher walked over by the window. When the teacher was in front of the window, the class perked up and listened intently. It wasn't long before the teacher remained planted in front of the window and finished his lecture from that side of the room.

This is exactly what I'm suggesting—when he's "by the

window," *communicate* to him that he's moving in the right direction.

The target is greater satisfaction for both of you.

Lighting It Up. . .Is That Okay?

What "acts" are permissible in the bedroom for a "good" Christian woman? Curious wives want to know.

Can we talk about this? It's a hot topic, and one on which you'll get many differing viewpoints. The reason for the conflicting opinions is that the Bible doesn't specifically address what a husband and wife can do in the privacy of their sexual relationship. Unfortunately, many feel guilty for certain actions and wonder if they've done something wrong. God gives us a clear restriction of no sex outside of marriage, but within marriage He instructs us to "imbibe deeply" (Song of Solomon 5:1). Where the Bible is silent, we need to be silent as well.

Let's look at where the Bible does speak.

Does it involve someone else? Watching X-rated, pornographic material that involves someone else would be outside of marriage and therefore is prohibited.

Some people have fantasies of bringing others into their bedrooms. Sex with someone you're not married to would be adultery. Even though your spouse might be there, it's still outside of marriage. Women have been pressured to engage in this type of "play" and may comply because they want to please their husbands. You may need to get counsel on this issue—if it becomes an issue—as you talk it through with your husband.

Another issue that can divide couples is whether or not anal sex is permissible. This one is more of a personal matter, and some may feel as though it is totally fine. Personally, I feel it should be avoided. Anal sex can cause tears and pain and a visit to the doctor. I can't see any reason to take a voyage there when a smoother voyage is only inches away. Again, my personal opinion. If this is something you're being pressured to do and you really don't want to, be very clear about how you're feeling.

A while back a young woman named Emily set up an appointment to talk with me. She was about to be married and wanted to talk about what to expect. Once we sat down, I could tell by her hesitancy and shy grin that she wanted to talk about sex. I let her know she wouldn't get any judgment or side-eye looks from me.

She took a breath and said, "My wedding is in less than a month, and I was wondering about a few things."

"How exciting!" I said. "I'm glad we found a time to talk."

Emily said, "I was wondering if oral sex is okay."

"What do you think?" I inquired.

"Well, I'm not sure. Someone told me you could get throat cancer, and that it was wrong."

I chuckled. (Later I did do some research on this, and apparently it is possible. Throat cancer is somehow connected through the HPV virus, but the risk is very small. Those most at risk, as with any sexually transmitted disease, are people who have multiple partners.)

Then I asked, "Have you read the Song of Solomon? Reading through that book, it's hard to make a case that it's wrong. But you and your husband will have to decide together. Basically, if it's okay with him and it's okay with you, then it's okay. Whatever you want to do is between you two. God doesn't explicitly say what we can or cannot do within the confines of marriage. So do what you feel is okay with you."

These types of conversations need to be had with the young ladies headed down the aisle. We tend to skip sex talks because we're embarrassed, but sex is a huge part of the marriage covenant and one that needs to be discussed.

No matter how long you've been married, be willing to talk

about likes and dislikes and be willing to respect the ideas and opinions of your spouse. What you find permissible is entirely up to you. What you choose to do in the privacy of your bedroom is between you and your spouse.

If you want to bring feathers or *whatever* into your marital congress, if it tickles your fancy, then go right ahead.

If you want to. . .

- use something that requires batteries or electricity or solar power
- enjoy watching him dangle from a pull-up bar dressed like Spiderman
- act like monks who have taken a vow of silence
- pretend to be Adam and Eve
- allow him to swing you around with his Superman cape
- use the tie on your robe like a sweat band or for *whatever*
- pretend to be Optimus Prime
- scream "Hallelujah!" when you like something
- lather up in chocolate syrup
- give him a chauffeur hat and "take it to the car"
- hang from a disco ball
- wear a Darth Vader costume

. . .it's entirely up to you and him. Light it up however you want to.

I'm not judging.

The next time your husband wants to do something that causes you to pause, ask yourself, *What is causing me to resist? Do I think this is dirty or inappropriate for a "good woman"?* If your reason for wanting to say no is unsubstantiated and comes from faulty beliefs, you may want to reconsider. Be reasonable.

However, if something could cause injury, infection, disrespect, or shame, you have a sound reason to pass. If you feel uncomfortable with anything, talk with your husband about your feelings with understanding and respectfulness. Be careful not to humiliate him in the process. Explain your objection kindly and reasonably. Be willing to talk about it and view it from his perspective. In the end, if you need to say no, a loving husband will understand and be willing to come to an agreement you both feel comfortable with. Most men will be happy with the many pleasures you're saying yes to.

Decide as a couple how you want to enjoy each other. What works for one couple may not work for another, which is why we need to create our own sexual practices. "All things are lawful for me, but not all things are profitable. All things are lawful for me, but I will not be mastered by anything" (1 Corinthians 6:12). Balance is imperative.

A wife contacted the well-known psychologist Dr. Kevin Leman for advice. She had found her husband masturbating in the shower and referred to him as a "sexual pervert."

This was Dr. Leman's response:

> The next time *you see him masturbating in the shower (or anywhere), throw off your clothes and say, "Honey, can I be of service to you?"* Masturbating is not the end of the world. You're not going to grow hair between your fingers. You're not going to go senile. All those things are flat-out lies.
>
> About 94 percent of men admit they masturbate. The other 6 percent are downright lying. Lots of women masturbate. There's nothing wrong with masturbation as a physical act. It's a release for sexual tension.

But because the imagination is connected with masturbation, it can become a major problem. If he's thinking about you and what he'd like to do with you at your next sexual interlude, there's nothing wrong with his thoughts. But if, instead of thinking about you, he's thinking about the newest little item who just started working at his office, that's a problem. Also, if your husband is using the sexual release of masturbation to soothe his sexual needs, and then he's too pooped to whoop with you, that's a problem.[1]

A wise woman will do whatever is possible not to cause shame or embarrassment for her husband. There are many differing opinions from many godly men and women on this subject. And many differing opinions among the experts as well.

What I would like to focus on is making sure this subject does not come between you and your spouse. I don't always agree with my husband on every issue, but I respect his opinion and honor his personhood. My honor for him does not change based on whether or not we are in agreement.

Never allow sexual issues or preferences to divide you. Work diligently to come to a compromise. You may need to agree to disagree, but be sure to stay unified as a team.

Husband and wife come together as one. In your physical relationship, work as one unit. In other words, you have four hands, and all hands are free to roam anywhere.

Let Your Hair Down and Let Loose

One of the best fictional scenarios involving a fantasy I've ever seen appeared on the TV sitcom *Modern Family*. A married couple, characters Phil and Claire, decide to be a bit adventur-ous on their Valentine's evening date by doing some role playing. Phil, wearing a name tag reading "Clive," sits on a stool waiting for his wife, Claire, playing "Julianna," to return from the ladies' room. She walks up to "Clive" wearing a trench coat and makes it very clear she's not wearing anything *but* the trench coat, and suggests they go to their hotel room.

Phil says, "This is so much better than cheesy garlic bread."

Arm in arm they get on the escalator, but then Claire's coat gets caught. With exasperation she says, "Phil! Phil! My coat is stuck!"

He says, "Who's Phil?"

She replies, "No! Not now, seriously, my coat is stuck."

Understanding their dilemma, Phil says, "Oh, oh, take off your coat."

"Are you kidding me?" she shrieks, then says, "Pull it! Pull it!"

Phil pulls with all he has but is unable to release her. As they reach the top of the escalator, Phil dives and hits the red button. The conveyor stops.

Phil then addresses the people behind them: "Come on up. Treat them like they are regular stairs. Happy Valentine's Day."

Just when you think the situation can't get any worse, they start running into people they know and multiple inquiries of why she won't just take off her coat.

Phil shoos them all off by saying the maintenance team is on their way. Finally alone but still stuck, Claire says, "That was the most embarrassing moment of my life."

Then. . .Claire hears the sound of her dad's voice calling her name. Jay, Claire's dad, and Gloria, her stepmother, just happen to be celebrating Valentine's Day as well. When Jay sees her par-alyzed against the hand rail, he asks, "Are you naked under that coat?" Realizing she is, he says, "Oh jeez!"

Gloria jumps into action and says, "It's okay, I got this." Gloria takes her own coat, puts it around Claire, and then helps her out from the trench coat, which is jammed tightly in the conveyor.

Claire says, "Thank you."

Gloria responds, "It has happened to me before."

Phil comments to Jay, "That's impressive."

Jay says, "Take it down a notch, Clive."

Claire's trench coat is left lying wedged in the gap between the stairs and the landing platform.

I found this to be one of the sweetest moments on TV I've ever seen. Gloria didn't shame her. She didn't lecture her. Nor did she say anything embarrassing. Instead, she said, "It has happened to me before," giving full acceptance and understanding.[2]

Well. . .this is me offering you my coat in sisterhood support. Free yourself up. No judgment. No embarrassment. Full acceptance. Embrace and explore your sensuality. Be adventurous. Offer yourself fully. Allow him to sweep you off your feet. Whatever that means for you. Together.

SECRET SEX MISSION #11

This is your mission if you wish to accept it: Words are powerful. Use them to build up your husband by praising his talents and expressing how much you enjoy bam-bam in the ham with him. Share what ramps up your desire. Do you have a fantasy? You only need to share it with one person—your husband. Step out and share it with him. Don't get upset if he doesn't respond in the way you'd like. He may laugh, only because he is not used to you communicating such a thing. But don't let that, or anything else, deter you. Communicate *clearly* what it is you want, and be persistent in making it happen. You'll be glad you did, and so will he.

ASK HIM

Be bold and ask him if he has any fantasies he'd like to try.

CHAPTER 12

SEXUAL AND GODLY

> NOT TONIGHT, HONEY—
> I NEED TO CUT MY TOENAILS.

There goes your sex life!" That's what I overheard another man say to my husband when he became a pastor. The image is burned in my memory, this well-educated but very ignorant professional laughing at my husband with the smugness of a bully on the playground. Mike grinned and calmly said, "I don't think so." That misinformed vocal man couldn't have been more wrong. What I wanted to say to him, but didn't because I was so taken aback by his brashness, was, *Listen, Bub, you have no idea. Sex just got even better. Boo-ya. [Insert mic drop.]* He had no clue that a relationship with God can blow up your love life.

The idea that *godly* and *nonsexual* go hand in hand is one of the biggest misperceptions of our culture and couldn't be further from the truth. Somehow the world equates being godly with being nonsexual. And if we're honest, we may do a little of that as well. Could it be that we have adapted some of the negative connotations our culture has attached to sex and sexuality? Sex has been used to exploit women and children, ruin marriages, spread destruction, and hurt innocent people. It's no wonder we may feel as though something is wrong with fully cutting loose. We've allowed the sexual climate of our culture to cloud God's glorious kaleidoscope of adventure and fun.

When we as women are perceived as sexual, we can feel we are doing something wrong. I was working in my husband's office at church and needed a break, so I walked across the street to get some coffee. As I walked down the busy sidewalk, some guy cat-called me. I looked because I thought it might be my husband joking around with me. But. It. Wasn't. Initially, I felt like I had somehow done something wrong. My first thought was, *Am I dressed appropriately?* Now, you need to know *I'm a grandma!* and the dress I was wearing was long sleeved and below my knees. I started thinking about how the world has perverted what God made to be beautiful and lovely and enjoyed. At times women can be made to feel like objects for sexual gratification, and that can cause us to want to reject sexual feelings completely.

We can come up with countless reasons to say no to amorous congress and be completely justified. Sometimes we're just tired or frustrated or not feeling good about ourselves. Sometimes we just don't want to. Period. I get it. I really do. Oftentimes, cake sounds more fun than sex. The difference between cake and sex is that after cake I almost always wish I hadn't eaten it, but with sex I can't think of a time I regretted it. Ever. Can you? Think about how you'll feel *after.*

The concept of an active and flourishing sexual connection with your husband can seem indulgent and frivolous. On our wedding nights, it feels like a big green light shines with approval, but later, frequent "indulgence" can feel like overdoing it. Certainly, there are more important things we need to be doing— who has time for personal indulgence? Counterfeit alternatives to fulfill our longings for intimacy can emerge in the way of idols, the pursuit of material things, an overinflated sense of self, or a quest for accolades and importance.

All lies from the enemy. The stronger our marriages are, the stronger witnesses of God's love we can be. The older I get the more deeply I understand this principle. Our marriages can be used by God to glorify the kingdom. I was married for many years before I learned to live under God's purpose for my life.

I've often heard women say, "I don't know what God's will is for my life." This statement sometimes puzzles me when made by a married woman. We tend to complicate things. If we're married, God's will is that we love our husbands—all out—emotionally and physically. "Above all, keep fervent in your love for one another, because love covers a multitude of sins" (1 Peter 4:8). God also wills that we *enjoy* our physical relationships with our husbands; it's one of His gifts to us. When I learned this truth and developed a deeper relationship with God, my physical relationship with my husband began deepening. "I didn't know it could be this good" has been a common theme as the years have gone by.

Here is how it all started. . . .

My Story

When I got married, I didn't believe in God. And sex? Yeah, it was happening, and it was pretty good, but I always felt like I was doing something wrong. I carried around a sense of guilt. Liking sex felt like I was somehow a *dirty girl* and doing something sinful. But if I looked at it as an obligation, something I had to do since I was married, then I could accept myself a little better. And the weird part about this was that I really wanted to enjoy it, but frankly, I preferred pizza to any slippin' and slidin'. I remember as a virgin thinking that sex was going to be the greatest thing ever and then was quite disappointed at the lack of magic and erogenous luster—those things would come later in my marriage, but I'm getting ahead of myself here. . . .

I grew up the daughter of an atheist. From the time I could talk, I can remember Dad telling me, "When you're dead, you're dead. They're going to put you in the ground. You didn't know anything before you got here, and you won't know anything when you're gone." As you can imagine, nights were difficult as a child. Life felt hopeless.

I figured when I became an adult, had my own love story, and got married, then I would fill the gnawing hole in my heart. Somehow growing up, falling in love, and "adulting" would fulfill my longing. After getting married at age nineteen, I discovered my longing only grew stronger. Instead of fixing my life, marriage brought more unfulfilled yearnings. Our marriage stunk. It was explosive and emotionally painful, and good moments were sadly elusive.

I felt stuck.

I felt hopeless.

I felt desperate.

I cried out to God and told Him I didn't believe in Him, but if He was real to please reveal Himself to me. God did. He showed up every day. I felt His presence. I became aware of my own sin. I became aware of my need for God. I knew I had to give Him my life and ask Jesus to take over and be my Savior. I invited Jesus Christ into my life as my ruler, boss, Lord. As Romans 10:9 says, "If you confess with your mouth Jesus as Lord, and believe in your heart that God raised Him from the dead, you will be saved."

I prayed something like this: *Lord Jesus, I believe You died on the cross for me. Forgive me for all my sins. I make You Lord, Master, and Ruler of my life. Come into my heart and my life and take over. I will live for You to the best of my ability from this day forward. Thank You for giving me eternal life, forgiving me, saving me, and loving me.*

In one glorious moment, I was no longer the daughter of an atheist. I became the daughter of the King of the universe. I live today as royalty, knowing I am completely loved by the almighty God. Life has never been the same. God gave me purpose, joy, hope, and a restored and loving marriage. He changed me.

Dealing with Guilt and Shame

God gives us freedom to love all out in every way. Guilt and shame are not from God. I know sometimes we can carry past relationships and *experiences* into our marriages. Women have told me they are haunted by past encounters, and those shameful memories intersect with their present, keeping them from fully indulging in their sexual relationship with their husband. If you have this problem, consciously clear your mind and visually imagine erasing each unwanted memory. You may need to talk with your husband to release any harmful baggage. When we talk about our feelings and are offered understanding and empathy, shame gets suffocated by love and acceptance.

Because of God, those past encounters *are* erased, and we can let them go. If you need to, ask the Father daily to release you of anything negative you're dragging with you until you feel complete freedom.

Soak in the words of Romans 8:1–4: "Therefore there is now no condemnation for those who are in Christ Jesus. For the law of the Spirit of life in Christ Jesus has set you free from the law of sin and of death. For what the Law could not do, weak as it was through the flesh, God did: sending His own Son in the likeness of sinful flesh and as an offering for sin, He condemned sin in the flesh, so that the requirement of the Law might be fulfilled in us, who do not walk according to the flesh but according to the Spirit."

The magic and erogenous luster that were lacking in the early days of my marriage began to be realized twofold after I fully grasped that I didn't need to carry guilt for delighting in the joys of intimacy that God created.

If you know Jesus, you can live in freedom.

If you know Jesus, you can live in sexual freedom.

Sexual and *Godly* Do Go Together

A deeper relationship with God can be a bridge to greater intimacy with your husband. *Sexual* and *godly* do go together—because God created us, and God created marriage and sex. Elisabeth Elliot says in *The Mark of a Man*, "You can't be human and not be a sexual creature. You can't be human and not be made in the image of God. You can't be human and not be a bearer of mystery. You can't be man in relation to a woman and not be skirting very close to one of the deepest mysteries of all."[1]

And what a beautiful mystery it is. Great sex comes from God. Unless you know the Creator and follow His instructions, you are only getting a watered-down version. Married sex is the best sex. Magazines and media will tell you to sleep around outside of marriage. You don't need to read articles or look to others; all you need to do is read the Bible. Only the Creator can instruct you on great sex. The closer you are to God, the better your love life will be. God gives you the ability to love to your fullest capacity and enjoy that love.

God designed man and woman to join together as one and become a family. The family unit is very important to God. Our relationships with the almighty Father are the foundations from which our marriages will flow. When my husband and I became Christians, our whole relationship—everything about it—became so much better. And do you want to know the best part? Our "interior decorating" totally ramped up.

The more we love God, and the deeper our relationships with Him, the more we will magnify Him and treat others with love. Notice that I didn't say we would *always* do things right or *never* act unbecomingly, but we will have a heart for reconciliation, and we will make amends by asking for forgiveness when needed. Sister, I'm not pointing fingers. I'm the queen of *Oops!* and apologies. Oftentimes it is what we do after we make a mistake that matters the most. A godly woman is marked by a pattern of love, respect, honor, grace, mercy, and a heart that seeks forgiveness.

In Romans 13:7-8, the apostle Paul tells us, "Render to all what is due them: tax to whom tax is due; custom to whom custom; fear to whom fear; honor to whom honor. Owe nothing to anyone except to love one another; for he who loves his neighbor has fulfilled the law."

WHAT HE WANTS YOU TO KNOW:

"Sometimes the only place I feel safe is in your arms."

—Kevin, very happily married husband

We need to connect being sexy, sexual, and sensual with being godly. Godly people exemplify love. We reveal how devoted to God we are—how godly we are—by our actions. We show it through the way we treat those around us *and* through the way we treat our husbands. Show me a woman who treats her man like God instructs, and you are looking at a godly woman. A woman who demonstrates love, respect, honor, grace, and mercy toward her husband exemplifies God. God is love. "Therefore be imitators of God, as beloved children; and walk in love, just as Christ also loved you and gave Himself up for us, an offering and a sacrifice to God as a fragrant aroma" (Ephesians 5:1-2).

WHAT HE WANTS YOU TO KNOW:

"Most men need to know that they are respected and heard. Men 'need' to feel needed and wanted."

—Anthony, husband, age fifty-five

Married to a Prince

Every man deserves to feel desired, needed, and built up. As a wife, you hold the reins to give your husband all that God desires for him to have in marriage. It matters to me that my husband prosper and shine and be every bit of the man God intends him to be. And I have a part in that because I can either function by God's instructions or resist and fight with God. I learned early on that resisting God never turns out well. For anyone.

Do you want a husband who's your prince, hero, and conqueror? If your husband is not that already, treat him as such, until he believes it and you believe it. When we are treated like we are valuable and cherished, we will believe it and act accordingly. Some of you may be thinking, *I've been treating him the best I can, but my husband is no prince.*

The straight and tricky truth is that sometimes it takes time. The kind of time you need God to help you be patient with. I wish relationships were like a vacuum and we could just plug them in and suck up all the bad stuff instantly. But the truth is, it could take years. A great relationship is more like a tree—it takes years to grow to maturity. It *may* happen quickly. You could see results faster than you thought, but you need to focus on committing until the end.

It was God who taught me how to be a wife. I know that sounds sappy, like I'm trying to be mega-spiritual or high and mighty—*Look at me, everyone—I'm buddy-buddy with God*—but actually His instruction came about after I'd hit rock bottom and experienced utter despair. I had nowhere else to turn. I felt desperately alone. My mother wasn't a Christian, and my marriage was so bad I didn't feel like I could put actual words to our situation and talk to anyone. When conflict arose between me and my husband—which was often—I picked up my Bible and asked God what I should do. I prayed and searched the scriptures. When I asked, He answered. *Always.*

Sometimes I would stumble on a passage and then become angry because I didn't want to do what it said. Many times the Lord's instructions didn't make sense to me, and I fought following them. But then I'd adopt a *whatever* mind-set and decide to trust. *Whatever*, because on my own I was messing everything up, so even though God's words seemed puzzling, I trusted and followed, hoping they would prove true. When we honor God, He blesses us. I have found this to be true in life and in my marriage.

Most people will respond favorably when they are treated well. I've heard men say, "My wife treated me so well, I just had to get my act together and treat her better." I can't tell you how long it will take, but most men will respond to love, admiration, and "parallel parking." Growing a tree takes time, but it will be beautiful in time. Doing things God's way is always worth it in the end. Proverbs 12:4 tells us, "An excellent wife is the crown of her husband, but she who shames him is like rottenness in his bones."

WHAT HE WANTS YOU TO KNOW:

"Like Atlas, we have the weight of our families on our shoulders."

—Gary, hardworking husband and father

The Marathon

Tyler loved to run. He could run for hours and hours. And when he wasn't running, he was thinking about running. His biggest dream was to run a marathon. Tyler trained faithfully, running miles each day. He did hill repeats, speed work, and intervals. After years of training, he decided he was ready to enter a marathon. Finally, his opportunity came. Feelings of elation surged through him as he imagined what that day would be like. The morning of his race, he was excited beyond compare.

But Tyler had one giant obstacle. He needed a special some-one to serve as his cup holder and be there for him at the designated aid stations. This marathon was different from others in that each runner picked one exclusive person to support them. Tyler selected his cup holder with extreme care, for this person would be the one who held out the water he would need through the marathon. On his big day, he felt confident he had chosen the right cup holder.

When Tyler lined up with the thousands of other runners, he nervously scanned the many people on the sidelines but couldn't find his cup holder. He decided to start the marathon anyway. This was his big day. Nothing was going to stop him from running.

At the first water stop, Tyler's cup holder was nowhere to be found. The holder had slept in that day and didn't make it to the first stop in time. Tyler kept running. Nothing was going to stop him, not even the absence of water at the first stop. He was thirsty but kept running.

At the second water stop, Tyler was excited to see his cup holder, relieved he would finally get some water. But his cup holder was socializing and didn't see Tyler run past. Tyler was so focused and determined to finish, he kept running.

At the third water stop, Tyler could see his cup holder from far off. Excited he would finally get some water, he ran faster than ever. As he approached, he could see his cup holder eating a big juicy burger and fries. But there was no water for Tyler. Even though he was wheezing and parched, he kept running.

As Tyler ran, he could not understand why his cup holder was being so insensitive. Etched in his mind was the cadence of the cup holder dipping fries in ketchup.

Perhaps the next stop would be the one.

When Tyler got to the fourth water stop, his cup holder was

reading a book, completely uninterested in Tyler and his need for water. At the fifth water stop, Tyler's cup holder was napping. *Napping.* Tyler could hardly believe his eyes. The pain in his body as he gasped for breath and his desperate need for water paled in comparison to the pain of being unloved and forgotten.

The next water stop. . .no water.

And the next water stop. . .no water.

And the next. . .

And the next.

While others around him were drinking water, there was none for Tyler.

Finally, Tyler got to the end of the marathon. Swallowing felt as if he were inhaling chunks of sand. Exhausted, frail, and brokenhearted, he crossed the finish line. This special day, which started out as the best day of his life, had turned into the worst day of his life.

In the crowd, Tyler spotted his cup holder. Hopeful he would finally get the water he urgently needed, he meekly asked, "Can I please have some water?"

Not paying much attention, his cup holder flippantly headed toward Tyler. Not being careful at all, this chosen person tripped, and the cup fell to the ground. Tyler ran over and picked it up, but all the water had spilled out.

The cup was empty.

In this fictitious marathon story. . .

The cup holder symbolizes a wife.

The water represents sex.

What's a Wife to Do?

If sex seems like a chore for you, focus in on what you like about the closeness you share, and allow yourself to enjoy this closeness. The key is making "baking lasagna" enjoyable for you too.

Find out what you like. Explore and be adventurous and go all out.

Now, you don't need to (nor should you) give a play-by-play of all the "moves" you didn't like. The way to approach this is with wisdom and care. Build him up as you voice your wishes. For example: I like. . . I like. . . I love. . . I *really* love. . . I'd like to try. . . And so on. As we discussed in chapter 9, you don't want to hurt him or cause him to shut down, so be sensitive to his feelings and tread carefully.

Our husbands are in the marathon of life. As wives, we can use our bodies as weapons against our husbands, hurting them emotionally by teasing and then pulling away, or by seeking to exert control through manipulative tactics. Or. . .we can use our bodies to refresh and restore our husbands.

The choice is ours.

The next time your husband approaches you for sexual congress and you are straight up just not in the mood and really don't want to, ask yourself, Why? Disinterest in sex on your part may indicate a relationship problem that needs to be addressed and fixed. Are you tired, overwhelmed with tasks, feeling emotionally wounded, or physically ill? If you're feeling hurt by something he said or did and it's keeping you from wanting to get close, take time to talk it through with him. If you're sick or in pain, make sure you let him know before he gets his hopes up.

WHAT HE WANTS YOU TO KNOW:

"I know you say yes to me 90 percent of the time, so I am very sensitive to you and pay attention to how you're feeling."

—Frank, sensitive husband

If you're feeling tired or overwhelmed when your husband makes an advance, ask for a *short* "monkey business" assembly. As a bonus, sex will help you sleep better. Have you ever woken up in the middle of the night and felt hugely frustrated because you couldn't get back to sleep? A roll in the sheets just might help.

Saying Yes

Think back to when you were in grade school and the teacher singled out two team captains to pick their teammates. Do you remember how good it felt when you were finally chosen? We all want to be chosen. When you're feeling like you want to say no, remember, all your husband wants is to love you. He is choosing you. He is choosing you above everything else, above anything else he could be doing. He's choosing *you*. Maybe you were the last one chosen back in grade school. Well, now you are being chosen *first*.

When you say yes, you are choosing to feel closer to him, to feel loved, to feel *chosen*. I promise you there will be times when the last thing you'll want to do is a bit of tumbling, but once things begin to heat up, you'll feel completely differently. Give things time to heat up. Allow yourself to be chosen.

I made a pact with myself to always say yes to sex. . .if possible. I like to refer to this personal policy as "The store is always open." Not out of pressure, not out of obligation, as in "I'm married, so I owe my husband this," but because I know it's best for me. It's best for me that I have a thriving marriage. It's best for me that my husband feels fulfilled. It's best for me that my kids feel secure because their parents are frisky and flourishing. It's best for me for physical reasons. It's best for me because the more I say yes, the less I feel depressed. It's best for me because

God says so. It doesn't make sense, but it works just the way God ordained it.

This policy safeguards my marriage. If "the store is always open," I'm motivated to work on my marriage daily. I can't harbor any bitterness, ill will, or negative thoughts toward my husband. I can't allow myself to hang on to angry feelings. No woman wants to have sex with a man she is mad at or doesn't esteem highly. My policy prompts me to work on *me*—daily. I have to take care of my body. Sleep is a must. After all, we generally don't want to have sex if we don't feel good about our bodies or are overly tired.

A "just say yes" policy can secure a happy, thriving marriage and sex life—and a better *you*.

Cravings Fulfilled

By God's natural order of design, a woman's body was fashioned to receive. To receive pleasure, to receive security, to receive care. No matter how much you may want to change that fact, no matter how much you may not like it, that's just the way it is. By God's design, a man's body was fashioned to lead, to forge the way, to present strength. We can submit to the Father's structure or we can resist. It's through God's mystery—the mystery of two becoming one—that we will experience exceeding joy and limitless pleasure and divine exhilaration, both spiritually and physically. Indulge, receive, cling, and bask in love committedly and devotedly.

God made us with deep longings and cravings for intimacy. And He also made a way for those cravings to be fulfilled through the union of husband and wife. When we feel loved, cherished, and filled, we will have more love to give. And the more love we give, the more we will feel loved. "Beloved, let us love one another, for love is from God; and everyone who loves is born of God and knows God" (1 John 4:7).

A woman will feel most fulfilled when she loves fully and completely.

Your marriage is your journey, your adventure, your romantic tale. You craft *your* love story. We cannot control another person, but we can completely control ourselves. When two people come together, one affects the other. Change one, and the dynamic will change. The relationship will change.

And now, my dear sister, we've come full circle. In chapter 1 and at various stops, I've encouraged you to pray, and I'm encouraging you to pray once again. Ask God for every bit of what you want in your marriage. Ask Him for the sex life you dream of. Live in the blessing of God's design for marriage intimately, sexually, spiritually. Imagine all of your desires realized.

To revolutionize your marriage, take this final Secret Sex Mission challenge.

SECRET SEX MISSION #12

This is your mission if you wish to accept it: For one month, say yes to his requests for romantic fun. If he doesn't make any advances, let him know "the store is open." Make advances yourself. Be responsive and all in. Consider turning one month into "the store is *always* open." This kind of policy will renew your sexual vigor and *will* revolutionize your marriage. Say yes to sex. You'll put a smile on his face—and a smile on yours.

ASK HIM

Sit down with your husband and talk about ways to expand your adventures. Be open to his perspectives and work on scheduling more "fun time."

My prayer is that this book would set your marriage on fire, and that it would do the same for millions of others. My dream is that we'd see more and more lasting, loving forever marriages. Let's heat up marriages around the world, one marriage at a time, starting with yours.

Now go and make your life better. Make your husband's life better. Touch future generations for eternity.

APPENDIX

RESOURCE LIST

Books
Heath Lambert, *Finally Free: Fighting for Purity with the Power of Grace* (Grand Rapids: Zondervan, 2013).

Kevin B. Skinner, *Treating Pornography Addiction: The Essential Tools for Recovery* (Orem, UT: Growth Climate, 2017).

William M. Struthers, *Wired for Intimacy: How Pornography Hijacks the Male Brain* (Downers Grove, IL: InterVarsity, 2009).

Websites
Be Broken Ministries: www.bebroken.com
Helps men escape pornography and sexual addiction; ministers to broken relationships

Celebrate Recovery: www.celebraterecovery.com
A Christ-centered 12-step program

Freedom Begins Here: www.freedombeginshere.org
Helps people find freedom from porn addiction and other sexual sin

Hope Restored: hoperestored.focusonthefamily.com
Offers struggling couples hope and restoration through a marriage intensive getaway program

L.I.F.E. Recovery International: www.freedomeveryday.org
A Christian recovery program

Safe Families: www.safefamilies.org
Offers help to adults struggling with sexual issues and provides resources to assist parents in protecting their children

XXX Church: www.XXXChurch.com
Helps men and women struggling with online porn

ABOUT THE AUTHOR

Lucille Williams, national speaker and author, has ministered to couples and families for over 25 years. As a pastor's wife, Lucille dedicates her time to ministry, writing, mentoring, and providing resources on her blog at LuSays.com. Working alongside her husband who is the children's pastor at Shepherd Church in Porter Ranch, California, Lucille found widespread success with her first book *From Me to We*.

In her pursuit to safeguard marriages, Lucille has appeared on *Focus on the Family*'s radio broadcasts and magazine as one of their top-rated programs for "BEST OF 2018." She was also featured on KKLA's the *Frank Sontag Show* and GOD TV. Even with her writing and speaking achievements, she will tell you her greatest pride and joy is her family—her highest calling and ministry.

Lucille resides in Los Angeles with her husband of over 37 years, spending the majority of their spare time with their grandkids.

NOTES

Chapter 1: Let's Talk about Sex

1. Bob Berkowitz and Susan Yager-Berkowitz, *He's Just Not Up for It Anymore* (New York: HarperCollins, 2009), 66.

Chapter 3: Sex and Your Mind

1. Elisabeth Elliot, *Love Has a Price Tag* (Grand Rapids: Baker, 2005), 107.
2. *Rocky II*, directed by Sylvester Stallone (Chartoff-Winkler Productions, 1979).
3. Gary Chapman, *The Five Love Languages* (Chicago: Moody, 2015), 45.
4. Les Parrott, *Crazy Good Sex* (Grand Rapids: Zondervan, 2019), 56–67.
5. Gary Smalley and Ted Cunningham, *The Language of Sex* (Grand Rapids: Baker, 2008), 17.

Chapter 4: Intimacy Interrupted

1. John Gray, *Venus on Fire, Mars on Ice* (Coquitlam, BC: Mind Publishing, 2011), 61.
2. Gary Smalley and Ted Cunningham, *The Language of Sex* (Grand Rapids: Baker, 2008), 111.
3. Shaunti Feldhahn, *For Women Only* (Colorado Springs: Multnomah, 2013), 80.

Chapter 5: But I Hate My Body

1. John Eldredge and Stasi Eldredge, *Love and War* (Colorado Springs: WaterBrook, 2011), 190.
2. Ibid., 182–84.
3. Kevin Leman, *Under the Sheets* (Grand Rapids: Baker, 2010), 170.
4. Kevin Leman, *Sheet Music* (Carol Stream, IL: Tyndale, 2003), 144.

Chapter 6: When Abuse Is in Your Past

1. Dan B. Allender, *The Wounded Heart* (Carol Stream, IL: Nav-Press, 2018), 73.
2. Doris Van Stone, *No Place to Cry* (Chicago: Moody, 1992), 15.
3. Allender, *Wounded Heart*, 197.
4. Carolyn Ainscough and Kay Toon, *Breaking Free* (London: Sheldon, 2018), 140.
5. Steven R. Tracy, *Mending the Soul* (Grand Rapids: Zondervan, 2008), 151.
6. Henry Cloud and John Townsend, *Boundaries* (Grand Rapids: Zondervan, 2017), 43.

Chapter 7: A Day in the Life of a Husband

1. Gary Chapman, *The Five Love Languages* (Chicago: Moody, 2015), 125.

Chapter 8: Men Are Visual

1. *Seinfeld*, season 4, episode 16, "The Shoes," directed by Tom Cherones, written by Larry David and Jerry Seinfeld, aired February 4, 1993, on NBC.
2. Stephen Arterburn and Fred Stoeker, *Every Young Man's Battle* (Colorado Springs: WaterBrook, 2004), 87.
3. Stephen Arterburn, *The Secrets Men Keep* (Nashville: Thomas Nelson, 2007), 242–34.
4. Marla Taviano, *Is That All He Thinks About?* (Eugene, OR: Harvest House, 2007), 68.
5. Arterburn, *Secrets Men Keep*, 245–46.
6. Kevin Leman, *Sheet Music* (Carol Stream, IL: Tyndale, 2003), 54.

Chapter 9: When His Engine Is on Idle or You Want to Rev Things Up

1. Bob Berkowitz and Susan Yager-Berkowitz, *He's Just Not Up for It Anymore* (New York City: HarperCollins, 2009), 126.
2. Kevin Leman, *Under the Sheets* (Grand Rapids: Baker, 2010), 176.
3. Ibid.
4. Ibid. 76.

Chapter 10: Keep the Engine Running

1. Gary Smalley, *The DNA of Relationships* (Carol Stream, IL: Tyndale, 2007), 120.
2. Shaunti Feldhahn, *For Women Only* (Colorado Springs: Multnomah, 2013), 147.
3. Kevin Leman, *Have a New Husband by Friday* (Grand Rapids: Baker, 2009), 137.
4. Shaunti Feldhahn, *The Male Factor* (New York: Crown, 2009), 50.

Chapter 11: Sex, Pancakes, and What Women Want

1. Kevin Leman, *Under the Sheets* (Grand Rapids: Baker, 2010), 103.
2. *Modern Family*, season 1, episode 15, "My Funky Valentine," directed by Michael Spiller, written by Jerry Collins, aired February 10, 2010, on ABC.

Chapter 12: Sexual *and* Godly

1. Elisabeth Elliot, *The Mark of a Man* (Grand Rapids: Baker, 2007), 51.

Also Available from Lucille Williams. . .

From Me to We
A Premarital Guide for the Bride- and Groom-to-Be

Engaged? Soon-to-Be Engaged? Or Just Thinking about Building a Healthy, Vibrant, Godly Life Together as Husband and Wife? . . .

Marriage is not for the faint of heart.

From Me to We is a transparent, surprisingly honest, and widely informative guide that will inspire you to safeguard your marriage by tackling tough questions and issues before you say, "I do." Lucille Williams, pastor's wife and trained Prepare/Enrich Marriage Facilitator, offers straight-talk about marriage with unprecedented insight as well as challenges and discussion questions—a must-have tool for premarital counseling.

Paperback / 978-1-63409-863-2 / $14.99